# REVEILLE

*for*

# SIOUX FALLS

## A WORLD WAR II ARMY AIR FORCES TECHNICAL
## SCHOOL CHANGES A SOUTH DAKOTA CITY

*To those who know neither thee or me, yet suffered for us anyway*

# REVEILLE

>>>>> *for* >>>>>

# SIOUX FALLS

## A WORLD WAR II ARMY AIR FORCES TECHNICAL
## SCHOOL CHANGES A SOUTH DAKOTA CITY

*Lynwood E. Oyos*

*Professor Emeritus of History*

*Augustana College*

*THE CENTER FOR WESTERN STUDIES*

*AUGUSTANA COLLEGE*

*2014*

Publication made possible with funding by the Anne King Publications Endowment and Ronald R. Nelson Publications Endowment in the Center for Western Studies and by the National Endowment for the Humanities.

ISBN: 978-0-931170-97-3

Library of Congress Control Number: 2013958145

Number 14 in the Prairie Plains Series

The Center for Western Studies (CWS) at Augustana College is concerned principally with preserving and interpreting native and immigrant cultures of the Northern Plains. The Center promotes understanding of the region through its archives, library, museum and art exhibitions, publications, courses, internships, conferences, and forums. It is committed, ultimately, to defining the contribution of the Northern Plains to American civilization. Visit the Fantle Building for the Center for Western Studies, Augustana College, 2201 S. Summit Avenue, Sioux Falls, South Dakota, or contact CWS at 605-274-4007 • 605-274-4999 (fax) • cws@augie.edu • www.augie.edu/cws • Facebook • Twitter.

Design and production: Red Line Editorial
Cover Photo: Courtesy Siouxland Heritage Museums
Design elements: HorenkO/Shutterstock Images; GOLFX/Shutterstock Images

Manufactured in the United States of America

# CONTENTS

Acknowledgments                                                      vi

Introduction                                                        viii

1     Reveille for Sioux Falls                                         1

2     Prosperity and Problems                                        26

3     Command                                                        49

4     Ohm's Law and Dit-Dahs                                         61

5     Field Training and Field Work                                  84

6     Remembering the Weather                                        94

7     Race Relations                                                111

8     Women and the War Effort                                      125

9     Misdemeanors and Murder                                       137

10    Base Life Away from the Classroom                             145

11    Use It Up, Wear It Out, Make It Do, or Do Without             167

12    Victory and Draw Down                                         180

Notes                                                               195

Works Cited                                                         206

Index                                                               210

# ACKNOWLEDGMENTS

On July 12, 1973, a disastrous fire at the National Personnel Records Center (NPRC) in St. Louis, Missouri, destroyed approximately sixteen to eighteen million official military files. Included in the loss were the records of the 2nd Air Force. The records of the Army Air Forces Technical Schools at the NPRC were destroyed. Therefore, a significant reliance was placed on articles in the weekly editions of the school's newspaper, *Polar Tech*, on deposit in the Center for Western Studies at Augustana College, when relating activities at the Sioux Falls Army Air Forces Technical School (ATS).

Private First Class Arthur Johnson III, Toledo, Ohio, in his journal and memoirs, provides a detailed account of one soldier's experiences at the radio school. Paul Graves, who was assigned to the Permanent Party at the base when it first opened, provides a critical view of the base's leadership. Another valuable source was the Oral History Center at the University of South Dakota, Vermillion. The Center contains several taped interviews with a number of GI students regarding their experiences at the base. Other tapes provide the views of local residents towards the soldiers in their midst. *The Sioux Falls Argus Leader* was also a valuable source in expressing the views of location citizens. Alfred Lorenz, a local resident who took his radio training at the base, provided additional material concerning the ATS.

The Karl E. Mundt Historical and Educational Foundation and Archives, Dakota State University, documents Congressman Mundt's role in bringing the Army Technical School to Sioux Falls. R. Douglas Hurt, in *The Great Plains during World War II*, provides an excellent description of how the Great Plains states sought defense contracts beginning in 1941. Barbara Tuchman in *Stillwell and the American Experience in China, 1916-1945*, describes the weaknesses of America's armed forces prior to 1941. I am indebted to three Augustana College graduates who authored papers related to material in the book: Pearl Sumption Anderson (B.A., 1956), Jocelyn Archer (B.A., 1981) and Dr. Mary Jarratt (B.A., 1980). Marie Christopherson, a reporter for the *Argus Leader*, provides insights into life at the Air Base in *Driftwood In a Time of War*, published by the Center for Western Studies. Alan

Lathrop, in *South Dakota History*, describes Harold Spitznagel's role in arranging housing in Sioux Falls and Rapid City during World War II, and John Keegan's *The Second World War* provides a good summary of the new fighter aircraft's role in enhancing the longer distance B-17s, which could fly into Europe and not be subject to attacks from German aircraft.

The many photographs came from a variety of sources, but the majority from the archives of the Center for Western Studies. Elizabeth Thrond, the Collections Assistant at the Center, and Aaron Culey were responsible for extensive work with the photographs. Doug Uthe provided a number of declassified photos of the base and personnel activities. Other photos were taken from the forty-page booklet given to each student when he graduated from the school. The booklets had many characteristics that we associate with high school and college annuals. David Kemp and Jim Carlson also provided photos. The Siouxland Heritage Museums and Mikkelsen Library's Media Services, Augustana College, also provided valuable assistance in completing this book. Amy Nelson, Office Coordinator at the Center for Western Studies, aided in the preparation of the manuscript. Able assistance when I first began research for this book was provided by Dr. Harry Thompson, now Executive Director of the Center for Western Studies.

# INTRODUCTION

Appearing before a Congressional Committee in January 1939, General Henry H. "Hap" Arnold, chief of the Army Air Forces (AAF), said that the American Air Forces was a "balanced compound of three essential ingredients—airplanes, combat and maintenance crews and airbases." To have an effective fighting force, the foregoing three must be kept continually in balance. Unlike other elements of the Army, the Air Forces depended upon its bases for fighting power, training effectiveness and strategic mobility. Properly maintained bases were the core around which all air force operations revolved. They were the point from which all air missions started and to which they returned.

Each base, regardless of whether it was used for training or for combat, had to maintain facilities both for housing and sustaining its personnel and for performing air missions within the United States. Within the United States, these air bases had to be properly located for continental defense. Given the advances made in modern air warfare, the Army Air Forces was obligated to maintain a striking force for home defense. Each field had to be suitable for employment by bombardment, fighter and air support aviation. The defense mission also dictated that an additional number of fields should be located across the midsection of the continent as to permit quick movement of air units from one defense area to another. As a training organization, the AAF required bases geographically so fitted as to provide the most favorable weather for year-round operations.

Prior to the attack on Pearl Harbor, the AAF Technical Training Command had an objective of 100,000 graduates per year. After the attack, the goal was raised to 300,000 and ultimately the goal reached a rate as high as 600,000. By March 1943, eight new technical training stations had been rushed into operation. Construction costs soared under the expedited procedures. By September 1945, the eight new stations, with a combined housing capacity of 130,924 personnel, had cost over $129 million.

The roughly constructed facilities also caused hardships to the personnel so housed; respiratory diseases at Kearns, Truax and Sioux Falls were almost a constant problem during the winter months and inclement weather turned the partly completed bases into muddy bogs.

Assigned to organize and command the eight new technical training stations was Major General Walter A. Weaver, who was successful only by the mass leasing of civilian facilities. The new training stations were basic training stations located at Kearns, Utah, and Seymour-Johnson Field, Goldsboro, North Carolina; mechanics schools at Amarillo, Texas, Lincoln, Nebraska, Gulfport, Mississippi, and Greensboro, North Carolina; and radio schools at Truax Field, Madison, Wisconsin, and Sioux Falls, South Dakota.

During the four years that followed America's entry into the war, Sioux Falls became a changed city. Several decades earlier railroads played the key role in the city's development. The presence of the Army Technical School, where as many as 30,000 men trained together at one time and sought entertainment and relaxation when permitted off the base, would bring new wealth into the community, change social attitudes, stimulate construction of new homes and businesses, contribute to the first small industrial park using abandoned base buildings, and take advantage of the new airport runways and buildings created by the military. A key to the city's growth was the surge in population. Judee Koplow Epstein, a local woman who worked at the base, said the base and the radio school "made Sioux Falls. The economic impact was phenomenal. Everybody made money. People who were in dire straits before all of a sudden were very affluent."

In the summer and fall of 1941, there was a scattering of houses on the north side of Sioux Falls. These homes were on the flood plain that bordered the Big Sioux River. This area of grassland extended northward as far as the eye could see. The flood plain was interrupted by occasional clumps of trees; to the northwest the plain ended in a series of hills. For something to do during the summer and fall months, local teenage boys spent considerable time exploring the grassland during the dry years of the 1930s.

City engineers had dug two drainage ditches in this area, later followed by the construction of a spillway to help counter overflow from the Big Sioux River if it did go over its banks in the spring or during a rare rainy season. The boys would wade through the tall grass to walk on a gravel road that bordered the ditch, which the youngsters called the "Canal." In the shallow waters of the Canal, the boys looked for crawdads and frogs, stirred up the mud hens and occasionally tried their luck at fishing. When walking through the grassland, there were days when they caused a pheasant to take flight.

The youngsters, throughout much of the 1930s, did not realize that their idyllic playground would soon be gone. The first airport for Sioux Falls, privately owned, had been established in 1929. It was located at the southwest corner of Western Avenue and 41st Street in the city of South Sioux Falls. The airport was a private investment and operated under the name of Soo Skyways Incorporated. Soo Skyways offered flight training and private passenger and airmail service. The runways were comparatively short and had turf surfacing. Throughout the 1930s, support grew for a public airport at a site that could easily be expanded. Local citizens expressed great interest in having regular passenger service. The city purchased 120 acres of the aforementioned grassland north of Maple Street and west of Minnesota Avenue. Through a WPA project, sponsored by the city, a stone hangar and an administration building were constructed. The two runways, 150' wide and 4,500' long, had stabilized gravel bases and an asphaltic concrete surface. Sioux Falls' second airport was dedicated on September 15, 1939. Knapp Brown, who had been with Soo Skyways, was hired as airport manager. Mid-Continent Airlines provided regular mail service and two daily flights each way.

Excursions into the flood plain by the city's youth were coming to an end and in April 1942, the area was to be transformed into a large military installation that at its peak would house 27,854 men and women of the United States Armed Forces.

# Chapter 1

*Hearing that an air radio and communication school was going to be built, a local wit, Lars Badstead, said that the new air corps school would feature higher education.*

While several thousand people left the Northern Plains region during the Great Depression, Sioux Falls gained approximately 7,500 new residents. The city's population totaled 40,832 in 1940. Much of the city's economy continued to rely on the fertility of the surrounding prairie through the processing of livestock and products of the soil. As of 1940, it was also a trading center and the distribution point for products destined for towns in eastern South Dakota.[1] Sioux Falls, just fifteen miles from the Minnesota border, was a placid, agricultural community.

Its homogeneous population, the majority of whom could trace their ancestry back to northern Europe, continued to feel the lingering effects of the Great Depression. Many people were still unemployed, and there was a continued reliance on WPA projects and federal relief programs. Depression prices persisted into 1942. The cost of a Sunday dinner at a restaurant ranged from 40 to 55 cents. Just 31 cents plus tax enabled one to enjoy an evening movie at the Hollywood Theater. Young women could dance at the Arkota Ballroom for 35 cents; their male partners could do so for 62 cents. Hamburger could be purchased for 19 cents a pound. As the nation entered its third month of involvement in World War II, the civic leaders of Sioux Falls sought answers to two questions: How could the city best express its support for the war effort? What could be done to revitalize the economy?

The war in Europe and ensuing events in the nation's capital provided answers to these questions. During World War I, the majority of the defense industry was located along the East Coast of the United States. The role of air power in the opening years of the European conflict, 1939-1941, indicated that the United States must strengthen its inadequate air force if it was to become involved in the European conflict. The relatively flat land of the Great Plains with its limited population appeared to be an ideal site for training pilots and other aircraft personnel.[2] In late May 1940, President Franklin D. Roosevelt called for the production of 50,000 planes a year.[3] Acting on the advice of the War Department, on June 26, 1940, Roosevelt signed the First Supplemental National Defense Appropriation Act. This legislation provided a billion dollars for military mobilization, including $84 million for constructing air fields, military housing and coastal defense. South Dakota's Congressional delegation notified local chambers of commerce to campaign for a share of this appropriation which would mean jobs and payrolls, a way to stimulate an economy still suffering from the Great Depression. In February 1940, the War Department committed $8.5 million for the construction of an air base for bomber training at Rapid City.

## SEEKING A DEFENSE CONTRACT

In his important book *The Great Plains during World War II*, R. Douglas Hurt provides an overview of the competition for defense dollars among the plains states in 1942. The Sioux Falls press and South Dakota's Congressional delegation also directed their attention to the economic issue. The question they asked was, "Why does the state have little in the way of defense contracts?" Certainly, South Dakota lacked industrial facilities capable of being converted to war purposes, but there had been no systematic and concerted effort to secure military contracts. The press insisted that community leaders must show the federal government what facilities were available, even if inadequate.

Throughout January 1942, U.S. Representative Karl Mundt addressed considerable correspondence to Paul K. Meyers, Secretary of the Sioux Falls Chamber of Commerce, pointing out that if Sioux Falls were to prosper, its commercial class could no longer conduct business as usual. He suggested that Meyers invite twelve to fifteen businessmen to have lunch with Fred Chase, the War Production Board representative for South Dakota. Mundt believed that receiving defense contracts was the key to increased prosperity.[4]

Telegrams came from Representatives Karl Mundt and Francis Case urging "every community and the state to 'get busy' and 'strike while the iron is hot.'" The state's representatives pointed out that the federal government was definitely embarked on a policy of spreading out the orders to the "little fellows" and that South Dakota ought to be able to get a share of them.[5]

In the discussions that ensued, all of the thinking was directed toward war production, perhaps dye and tool production or a central assembly plant.[6] In a letter to Claude Hamilton, Department Commander of the American Legion, Mundt suggested that Hamilton and others explore the possibility of a Veterans' Administration hospital east of the Missouri River.[7]

On February 4, Representative Mundt informed L. F. Boyce of the Sioux Falls Construction Company that he would be present in Huron on Sunday, February 8, for a conference to explain what had been done and to answer questions. Two hundred men from twenty-four eastern South Dakota counties and three counties in southwestern Minnesota were in attendance. Conference speakers included Karl Mundt, Max Rysdon of Sioux Steel, Sioux Falls, and Fred Chase, Acting Director of the War Production Board with offices in Sioux Falls. After a temporary eastern South Dakota War Production Committee was formed, the conference considered the manner in which East River South Dakota facilities could be used in the defense program. The decision was made to assemble data on existing facilities in South Dakota and to present the information to the proper authorities.[8]

Ironically, the prior day, February 7, community leaders in Sioux Falls learned of the possible answer to their two questions. The city was under consideration as a possible defense facility. Major General Rush B. Lincoln, the former commander of U.S. Army Air Corps technical training with headquarters at Tulsa, Oklahoma, and members of his staff, dropped in at the Municipal Airport unannounced. The General and his staff attended a luncheon with members of the Chamber of Commerce to discuss establishing an Army Air Corps training school in the city. Two days later, February 9, Mayor John T. McKee, city engineer Reuben Bragstad and Paul Meyers left by plane for Tulsa, taking with them the data the general had requested. Returning three days later, they awaited the arrival of an Army site investigating board on February 13. This team of investigators remained in Sioux Falls for three days.

Fred Christopherson, editor of the *Sioux Falls Argus Leader*, who had attended a dinner with the team of investigators, informed Mundt, on February 16, that Sioux Falls would be recommended for a technical training school. Christopherson emphasized that the recommendation must be kept confidential because Senator George Norris, of Nebraska, "had the President's ear" and Norris wanted a technical training school for either Lincoln or Grand Island, Nebraska.[9]

To further promote the city's bid for an air base, Meyers, Bragstad and City Attorney Roy Burns traveled to Washington, D.C. In lobbying for Sioux Falls, they indicated that the city had an adequate supply of skilled and unskilled labor. There were many unemployed carpenters, masons and other construction workers available. They emphasized that having an air base would give the city a chance to participate in the war effort, and that it would mean a definite improvement in business and labor conditions.[10] Senator Chan Gurney wrote Meyers that he had contacted the Secretary of War and high ranking Army Air Forces officers, lobbying for the Sioux Falls site. Henry Carlson, a Sioux Falls contractor, received a letter from Mundt stating that it was safe to say that the air corps school was "in the bag" but that it was imperative that no public announcement be made because there were still bureaucratic stops to be made.[11] Hoping that the War Department would respond positively, the city began securing options from owners of large tracts of land near the airport.

## SIOUX FALLS GETS AN ARMY SCHOOL

Positive news came from the nation's capital on March 27, 1942. A banner headline in the *Sioux Falls Argus Leader* proclaimed, "IF LAND CAN BE PROVIDED, SIOUX FALLS GETS ARMY SCHOOL." Senators Chan Gurney and William J. Bulow and Representative Mundt jointly made the announcement in a telegram from Gurney to the *Argus Leader*:

> The War Department late this afternoon advised Senator William J. Bulow, Congressman Karl Mundt and myself that the Sioux Falls radio air communication school

had been completely authorized provided the city of Sioux Falls can secure legal options on all land and turn it over to the government under lease on or before April 3.

We here in Washington are advised that more than 90 percent of the land is now under option and we have, therefore, secured from the War Department complete permission to make public announcement with the thought that the announcement will be helpful in securing from the owners the balance of the needed land their immediate agreement for the sale of their property.

We here in Washington congratulate Sioux Falls on the opportunity to be a part of the national war effort.[12]

If the land were secured by the April 3 deadline, the War Department said it would establish a $15 million U.S. Army Air Corps Radio and Communication School on a 1,500 acre tract, including the Municipal Airport, and acreages northwest of the city. The training center would have facilities for 15,000 military personnel. It meant the addition of more than one-third to the city's population.[13]

## LAND ACQUISITION

Despite having only a week's notice, M. T. Woods, a local attorney and president of the Sioux Falls Chamber of Commerce, expressed confidence that all options on the land needed for the proposed air base would be secured by the deadline. He said that "Property owners in Sioux Falls have been very cooperative. They regard the coming of the school to Sioux Falls as a patriotic proposition and they have been willing to sell at fair prices. It is a commendable attitude when we consider that they are willing to give up their homes and undergo certain inconveniences to make way for this big school."[14]

A remarkable, all-out, community effort transpired within the next week. Although, as indicated, 90 percent of the options had been secured from tracts held by large property owners, there were a large number of small property owners from whom leases would have to be secured. A committee of twenty local lawyers, which included Woods, James O. Berdahl, Gail Braithwaite, C. A. Christopherson,

Raymond Dana, Claude Hamilton, Louis Hurwitz, Robert May, Gene Pruitt and chairman Roy Willy, scheduled a meeting for Monday night, March 30, with the remaining property holders. More than 400 people attended the meeting in the city hall auditorium. M. T. Woods had urged those coming to the meeting to bring with them deeds, abstracts, contracts and mortgages.[15] The city commission had authorized Mayor McKee and city auditor, C. M. Whitfield, to execute contracts and agreements for purchasing land. In purchasing property, the city was obligated to pay the purchase price of the land. The estimated cost to the city for acquiring the property and meeting other War Department requirements totaled approximately $500,000. At the meeting, the methods of payment for the property secured were explained. City attorney Roy Burns told the assembled group that the city must secure deeds to said property and property owners must sign escrow agreements. The assembled attorneys had to secure options from seventy-five different property owners. It was no small task. Owners of some of the parcels had died, leaving heirs at scattered sites. There were instances where no court action had been taken to vest property in these heirs.[16]

Dozens of parcels were placed in escrow in two hours. Real estate agents fixed values on 40 properties that were homes of people in the affected area. The home owners were to be paid a fair price for turning over their property. Don Cook, a Sioux Falls real estate agent and representative of the Getty Abstract Company, checked property records. By the close of the meeting, Burns announced that more than 98 percent of the land was now in the hands of the city. Only a few lots were outstanding when the attorneys reported on April 3 that the city held deeds to 99.7 percent of all the property needed for the air base. Of the 9.4 acres not under deed to the city, some had not been secured because of absentee ownership or unsettled estates. A few owners had placed an excessive and unacceptable price on their property. The government had the option of initiating condemnation proceedings for these remaining properties.[17] Mayor McKee announced that city attorney Roy Burns was prepared to present a resolution to the city commission incorporating the newly acquired property into the city limits, including the municipal airport. Members of the South Dakota Congressional delegation were contacted in hopes that the War Department would concur that all conditions had been met and that a favorable decision would be announced on Saturday, April 4.

In addition to the land acquisition, the War Department had studied the proposed project from every possible angle. Public facilities were examined, records of the climate had been obtained, recreational opportunities surveyed and the attitude of the citizens considered.[18]

Political and administrative people in the nation's capital were impressed with the success of the city's land acquisition effort. In a letter sent to the land acquisition committee, Karl Mundt noted, "You fellows certainly amazed Washington with the speed with which you got the land. Lieutenant Kuder told me today that the experiment that they made in Sioux Falls of announcing a project tentatively, subject to securing the land, worked out so surprisingly well that the War Department is considering making that their established instead of their exceptional practice."[19] Senator Gurney said that Army officials in Washington were impressed by the excellent job done in Sioux Falls to acquire the necessary land. The *Argus Leader* described it as an all-out sensational effort.

## BOND ISSUE

The property owners, who had surrendered their deeds, were to be paid following the city electorate's approval of a bond issue. If approved, the city would distribute funds needed to various Sioux Falls banks, holding the deeds in escrow. Property owners whose title had been approved would be paid as soon as the funds were in hand.[20]

Voters were asked to approve a $500,000 bond issue at an election scheduled for April 21. A 60 percent majority was required for passage. Speaking to members of the Chamber of Commerce, Burns said the city would pay off the bonds at a rate of approximately $35,000 a year over a fifteen-year period. The cost for city residents was less than $1 per year in taxes on each $1,000 of assessed valuation. He reported that the interest rate would be less than 2 percent when the bonds were sold. The current bonded debt of the city was less than $500,000, with the bonds having been reduced regularly.

The *Argus Leader*, in a lengthy editorial, argued that "No One Should Vote Against the Bonds":

> A unanimous endorsement would be a great patriotic gesture. The projected air base was necessary for the economic welfare of the community. Young men, skilled workers and tradesmen had left the city. Businesses were

curtailed by shortages and rationing. Sixty percent of the city's out-of-town trade would decline with the rubber shortage. There were vacancies in rental properties. Home construction was limited because jobs and materials were not available. With an air base, hundreds of construction workers would be needed, and they would need housing and food. Money would be injected into the city's economy at cafes, theaters, and other sites of entertainment. The base would be self-liquidating. Once the conflict was over, the city would acquire the air base, meaning that Sioux Falls would have a source of water for years to come and expanded airport facilities.

The paper's editor concluded, "There is no valid reason for opposition on the part of any citizen irrespective of his or her occupation or position in the community."[21] In a large ad paid for by the citizens' Committee for Airport Bonds, two questions were raised: (1) When the war is ended and won, who will own the land and the airport? Answer. The city of Sioux Falls. (2) If the war is not won. Who will own the land? Answer. Hitler, Hirohito and company will control our airport and us.

As A. A. Isakson's house at 1408 N. Elmwood Avenue stood on jacks ready to be moved to lots on Lyndale Avenue between 14th and 15th streets, he commented, "I haven't heard a complaint from anybody who has to move. Everyone is anxious to do everything for the war effort and we are glad to get out if it will be of help in winning the war . . . . In spite of the inconveniences, I think everyone who sold their property was treated fairly–none of them have complained that I know of."[22]

Jay B. Allen served as general chairman of a citizens' airport bond committee. The committee wanted a 100 percent vote for the bond or as close to 100 percent as possible. Their slogan for the drive was, "Be Patriotic – Vote Yes 100 Percent." One of the large ads in the local newspaper read, "Vote to Lick the Axis Now and Have a Greater Sioux Falls When that Job Is Done."[23] Ralph Roberts was the general chairman of the publicity committee, and his colleagues were Joe Floyd, David H. Smith and Evans Nord. They named a ward chairman for each voting precinct.[24]

Two days before the election, City Auditor C. M. Whitfield reiterated that the city's bonded debt was at the lowest point in more than two decades. The city had retired $100,000 in water bonds and $75,000 in sewer bonds in July 1941. On January 1, 1942, Sioux Falls' bonded debt stood at only $519,255.50. Aside from the forthcoming bond issue, he did not foresee any other bond issues being floated in the immediate future. The editor of the *Argus Leader* wrote that "No thoughtful citizen will oppose the Bond Issue." He said there was no good reason, economic or patriotic, to oppose it.[25]

Although only 50 percent of qualified voters went to the polls on Tuesday, April 21, the bond issues received overwhelming support. The bond issue for $400,000 carried 8,785 to 981; 89.9 percent of the voters had favored the issue. The vote on the second issue for $100,000 was 8,785 to 1,094, with 88.6 percent supporting the measure.[26] The editor of the *Argus Leader* wondered why 50 percent of eligible voters refrained from voting. He wrote, "People who delegate responsibilities are engaging in a dangerous practice. They may delegate their privilege to the wrong person." Following a canvas of the vote, the city commission called for the issuance of the bonds on Monday, April 27. Adhering to state law, bids for the sale of the bonds had to be advertised for three weeks. Then the bonds would be sold to the highest bidder. The Acquisition Project Manager for the Army Corps of Engineers said it was "the cleanest and most smoothly running land acquisition that he had encountered in his experience with the War Department. The absence of the necessity for condemnation proceeding is an outstanding credit to Sioux Falls." The bids on the air base bonds were $100,000 less than the voters approved. The bonds were sold at an interest rate of 1.5 percent. In addition, the city received a substantial premium on the two issues.[27]

While the bond drive took place, other preparations for the base were made. On April 4, the War Department had officially announced that a U.S. Army Radio and Communication School, costing more than $15 million, would be established in Sioux Falls. It would eventually house 500 officers and 14,500 personnel. The Omaha Division of the Corps of Engineers would be ready to let contracts in thirty days. Construction was expected to be completed in 120 days. Once the base was functional it would have a monthly payroll of $600,000.[28]

## COLONEL CAMBLIN ARRIVES

On April 9, the officer who would be in charge of construction, Colonel Roy W. Camblin, arrived in Sioux Falls. An Air Corps veteran of nearly twenty-five years, he had been commissioned a colonel in January 1942. The native Texan had served at many air base installations, including three years in the Philippine Islands. His last posting before coming to Sioux Falls was Lowry Field in Colorado where he served as executive officer at an Air Corps Technical School. Camblin and his staff eventually found office space on the third floor of Sioux Falls City Hall in an area formerly occupied by the U. S. Employment Service. They would remain there until offices were erected at the Training School. Captain Donald Blair, engineering officer from the district headquarters in Omaha, along with a staff of a dozen engineers and architects, set up office in the Sioux Chevrolet Co. storeroom at Main Avenue and 11th Street. Plans and specifications for the first stages of the new school were to be completed by the end of the first week in May. Major E. E. Taylor, also from district headquarters in Omaha, was designated supervisory engineer in charge of construction. He recently had had charge of the construction of the Army bomber base in Sioux City. All plans and specifications were to be sent to Colonel Lewis A. Pick in Omaha. The completion date for construction of the new base was originally set for August 23.[29]

Colonel Camblin proposed that the new base be named George Field. George had been Camblin's close friend for twenty years. Brigadier General Harold H. George had accompanied General Douglas MacArthur on his flight from Bataan to Australia. George was killed in a plane crash in Australia in late April. The Chamber of Commerce, in support of Camblin's suggestion, made a formal request to the Army Air Forces headquarters in Washington, D.C.

The request was not approved and the new air base was called the Army Air Corps Technical Training Command (AACTTC) School.[30]

## LEASE AGREEMENT

The base was activated on April 10 when a representative from the Army Engineers Office, Mayor McKee and City Auditor Whitfield signed the lease turning over 1,540 acres for the training site. The lease granted the land to the federal government for $1.00 per year and gave federal authorities the right to renew for one year periods for the next twenty-five years. Commercial airliners continued to have the right to use the municipal airport. Private planes, with two-way radios, could use the fields under military restrictions.[31] The government was assured that the air base would have an adequate supply of water. Commissioner Joseph Nelson said there would be no shortage as the city would soon have three new wells in operation. The new wells would have a daily capacity of between four and five million gallons. Nelson estimated that the training school would use about two million gallons, about twice the amount the meat-processing plant John Morrell and Company used each day. He calculated that the government would pay the city approximately $60,000 annually for water.[32] The city held the right to construct new wells and maintain wells and pipes already on air base property. The tops of all the wells were to be flush with the ground.[33]

The agreement further stated that the city was to close all roads in the area of the school and reroute them. Lastly, the city was obligated to remove all buildings from the area leased to the government. House-moving crews began removing 172 buildings from the area on April 11. Brandt Engineering Company, with six crews at its disposal, estimated that it would take approximately thirty days to complete the task.[34] On May 1, the final twelve houses on the future site of the air base were being moved. The city, two days earlier, held an auction that included twelve houses plus garages, sheds and chicken houses. At 5:00 P.M., an hour before bidders arrived at the sale, a heavy rain began to fall. The rain was accompanied by winds reaching 55 to 60 miles per hour. Auction bidders who waded through the mud were not in a generous mood. The highest bid for a house was $750. The city netted a total of $2,824 from the auction.[35]

Thus, during the first week in May, the future site of the Army Air Base was a relatively quiet segment of the fertile Big Sioux River Valley. The river flowed lazily along the northwestern boundary of the future military reservation. To the south were the clear waters of Covell Lake. In the cultivated areas of the 1,500-acre tract there was a lush growth of rich, green grass and one could see a few trees. Within a few weeks, the area would be transformed into barracks, office buildings, classrooms, warehouses, hangars and extended runways—and 15,000 military personnel, more than one-third the population of Sioux Falls, would occupy the site. Personnel from the Corps of Army Engineers immediately developed detailed plans for constructing facilities on the cleared land. Estimating that construction would take four to five months, Colonel Lewis A. Pick, in charge of the Omaha District of the Army Corps of Engineers, began to award contracts for construction.

## HOSPITALITY

Civic leaders urged residents of Sioux Falls to welcome incoming military personnel. The *Argus Leader* in an editorial entitled "Sioux Falls Shoulders a Patriotic Task" declared:

> . . . It is our function to do all that we can to provide a wholesome and helpful atmosphere and to cooperate with the military authorities in every way possible in making this one of the finest army schools in the country. We can and should treat these incoming soldiers as we would want our sons, brothers and friends who are in the service elsewhere to be treated . . . . We should prepare to receive them as honored guests--as members of the grand company of American men who today are beginning to shoulder the brunt of the battle to maintain their nation's independence and security.[36]

Mayor John T. McKee commented, "Sioux Falls is glad to welcome the Army. This gives the city an excellent opportunity to take part in the nation's war program and I know every man and woman in Sioux Falls is more than anxious to do everything possible in prosecution of the conflict against our enemies."[37] Meyers, Secretary for the Chamber of Commerce, said that Sioux Falls had a big responsibility "to invite close to half of its population to come here within the next two to six months." Military personnel should be treated in such a way that when they leave they will feel that nothing had been left undone to make them happy and comfortable. He hoped that the YMCA, churches and other facilities would convert current recreation rooms into social centers for servicemen where the community's young people could meet them. Appealing to housewives, Meyers urged the setting up of a system whereby homes would invite one or two young servicemen to Sunday dinner. Speaking from experience, he said, "A home-cooked meal appeals to soldier boys more than anyone realizes."[38]

C. D. Rohlffs, Chairman of the City's Defense Council, invited representatives from all of the city's civic clubs to meet with him at the Chamber of Commerce on April 15 to coordinate activities for a city hospitality program.[39] The USO was asked to take quick action regarding the Air Radio Training School. The USO usually built a large clubhouse adjacent to a military installation that provided general recreation facilities.[40] Reverend Clarence W. Adams, as president of the Sioux Falls Ministerial Association, said that its members had pledged to meet the spiritual needs of the young men at the camp. They offered their churches for worship, friendship and recreation. Hopefully, the servicemen would enter into the full social life and fellowship of the respective congregations.[41] On May 18, the Church Council of First Lutheran Church approved the establishment of a service center at the church in cooperation with other churches in the city. The supervisory committee consisted of Dr. Melvin Mortrude, Stanley Olsen and Ralph O. Hillgren.[42]

The local civilian defense council, chaired by Joe Floyd, established two recreation committees. The Civilian and Service Recreation Division included a sub-division of private agencies that would provide recreation for selected groups of soldiers and civilians in conjunction with regular activities. The Soldiers' Recreation Division was confined to the interests of the airmen and the facilities that were available to cater to these interests.[43] The Ivory Room in the Carpenter Hotel was set aside as a social center for military officers. Before a USO was fully established, temporary headquarters were created at the Hollywood Theater. At this site, enlisted men found stationery, reading material, table-tennis tables, and board games.[44] On June 20, a USO site was selected. It was the Furniture

Mart Building at 116 S. Phillips Avenue. The Federal Security Agency supplied funds for its rental and equipment. Colonel Camblin approved the selection. He said the building was ideally located. It was "One of the most desirable in the city in which to establish a USO facility. The immediate establishment of the facility is of prime importance."[45]

## HOUSING ISSUES

Thorough in their preparations, community leaders called upon twenty realtors to study available housing in the city before the first contingent of service personnel arrived. They made a city-wide survey to ascertain what space was available. The realtors made a list of the houses for sale, rental units, apartments, office space for rent and rooms for rent in private homes.[46] They determined that there were twenty-four houses for rent and eighty-three apartment openings. A six-room house rented for $33 per month, a five-room unfurnished duplex rented for $35 per month. Unfurnished apartments rented for $30 while a three-room furnished apartment could be had for $45 a month.[47] The city commission approved an ordinance regulating non-permanent and portable dwellings occupied by project workers and transients in general. The ordinance imposed a ninety-day residence limit upon trailer occupants unless they were employed in vital defense work, in which case provision would be made for renewal for another ninety-day period. The commission asked people wanting to establish trailer or cabin camps within the city limits to make their intentions known as soon as possible.[48]

On May 1, only ten houses were listed for sale in the *Argus Leader.* Three- and four-room apartments were renting for $27-$28. Any thoughts of price gouging by some landlords ended suddenly on June 3 when the Office of Price Administration, headed up by Leon Henderson, froze apartment and house rental rates at the March 1 level. The order covered Minnehaha, Lincoln and Turner counties in South Dakota, Rock County in Minnesota and Lyon County in Iowa. The designated area was given sixty days to bring rents in line with the edict or a federal administrator would enforce them. One real estate agent commented that individual house owners had increased rents an average of 10 percent since March 1.[49]

Some landlords feared rents were being shoved down to "dust storm" levels. They argued that rentals were below normal levels on March 1. There were those who feared the landlord was "going to take a beating," and they complained about the high cost of repair materials. Single rooms were extremely scarce as they were being rented by craftsmen and laborers whose ranks would swell to nearly 5,600 men in June.

On June 11, a second city-wide survey was conducted by the Boy Scouts to determine the amount of living space available within Sioux Falls. During the morning, the Scouts assembled at the post office to receive instructions. Three Scouts accompanied each mail carrier on his route as he pointed out places where vacancies might exist. The Scouts returned in the afternoon to the places designated and checked on the type of housing available.[50] The Boy Scouts reported that there were approximately 448 rooms, houses and apartments available for rent at present or in the immediate future. With the Army planning to employ more than 2,000 civilians, including radio instructors, secretarial personnel, draftsmen and utility repairmen, when training at the base reached its peak, community leaders considered requesting defense housing.[51]

## CONSTRUCTION UNDERWAY

As construction began, Lieutenant Colonel Travis Hetherington, the assistant commandant and school director, appointed Detective C. J. Rufer of Sioux Falls as area protective security agent. Rufer was a former chief of police. Given a leave of absence from the police force, he served at the base until construction was completed. Rufer eventually supervised fifty guards whose duties were distributed over twenty-four hours. Many of the guards controlled the perimeter of the construction zone on horseback and barred the public from roads adjoining the training school area. Barricades were erected on the main roads. Because the Municipal Airport was under lease to the War Department, only persons going to the airport to board a plane and those going to meet passengers arriving on incoming planes were permitted on the property. Before the arrival of each plane, the airline furnished the guards with a list of outgoing and incoming passengers. Passenger service was temporarily suspended while construction was underway. Only air mail and air express were permitted during this time.[52]

Many local citizens could no longer engage in their favorite past-time of watching Mid-Continent airliners come in.[53] Anyone wanting to watch the progress of construction, could do so from Terrace Park. When the construction of the base was completed, Rufer and his men were replaced by Air Force personnel. The new military reservation was eventually surrounded by 6.8 miles of woven wire fencing.

As the Army began to let bids for the earthwork, grading and excavation, civic leaders were unduly concerned about potential labor problems. Labor difficulties had occurred in the construction of the bomber base at Rapid City and it was hoped that similar problems could be avoided at Sioux Falls. Earlier, the editor of the *Argus Leader* had commented: "It will be to the distinct advantage of everyone concerned if the labor relations angle of the camp construction be left in the hands of Sioux Falls leaders in the building unions who

Army Technical School and northwest Sioux Falls, South Dakota, July 1943. *Courtesy Siouxland Heritage Museums.*

have demonstrated already their reasonable attitude. The main task will be to prevent the entrance of outside agitators who may see this project as an opportunity to create discord and feather their own nests.[54]

The manager of the South Dakota State Employment Service said that in selecting workers, regulations required that Sioux Falls workers be selected first, then those from Minnehaha County and finally those from a greater distance. By mid-April, job hunters were filing through the Employment Service Office at a rate of 700 per day, more than twice the normal daily traffic.[55] Employment at the base steadily drained off qualified WPA workmen. It was estimated that 3,000 men in the Sioux Falls area enrolled in WPA projects during the worst depression years. As of May 31, only eighty-eight people were assigned to WPA projects in Minnehaha County. Of these workers, less than one-fourth were considered unemployable by private contractors.[56] It had been WPA crews that had constructed the airport administration building, a hangar and drainage system between February 1938 and November 1939. These facilities helped make it possible for Sioux Falls to gain a training school. When construction reached its peak in mid-June, local WPA projects were suspended. As of June 17, there were no employables asking for assistance, and relief expenditures, $6,135.00, reached their lowest level since the program was introduced in the 1930s.[57] Six construction companies joined to form the Sioux Syndicate, including Sioux Falls Construction Company and Norlin and Stadem's Acme Concrete Company.

Excavation work and the construction of a railroad spur track to the base had begun on April 27. Using fifteen to twenty scrapers, and two manpower shifts during a sixteen-hour day, engineers expected to complete the leveling of the base site in one week. Rain and hail, however, accompanied by strong winds began on April 28 and the rain continued for several days. Excavation and leveling stopped on the evening of April 30 as mud became the enemy. The normal rainfall for Sioux Falls for April was 1.54 inches. In 1942, rainfall totaled 4.44 inches. The rains continued into early May but engineers reported that run-off was good and operations continued after gravel was used to cover muddy areas.

Several residents living near the construction site complained about the noise of the trucks. The Army Engineer's office replied, "The sound of trucks is better than the sound of bombs." The noise was an inconvenience but a war was being fought and the school had to be finished as quickly as possible.[58] One of the major projects, as workers battled "General Mud," was the construction of a new runway, preceded by changing the channel of the Big Sioux River.[59] The existing northeast-southwest runway was to be abandoned and replaced by a runway that was 5,700 feet long. The northwest-southeast runway was lengthened to 5,700 feet. The new runway and the extension were built of a soil-cement stabilized base. The mixing of the two materials provided a good wearing surface.[60] Along the west side of the ATS, a large dike was erected to keep out possible high water from the Big Sioux River.

By the end of May, over 5,600 men were engaged in constructing the new Army installation. The work force included 507 laborers, 246 carpenters, 211 truck drivers and 51 scraper operators. In addition to the runways, this assembled force of manpower began construction of barracks, classrooms, administrative offices, a hospital, chapels, warehouses, hangars, a boiler house and a sewage disposal plant that was comparable in size and type to the city's municipal plant. Thirty miles of pipe were laid for the sewer and water system. Seventeen miles of bituminous surfaced streets were laid throughout the school area and 6.8 miles of fencing was erected around the base.[61] Contractors said the peak of construction would be reached in June.[62]

Army contractors used an assembly line to mass produce buildings at the training school: (1) The process began in the drafting room where the measurements, sizes and specifications for each piece of lumber were prepared. (2) The specifications were sent to the saw mill where pre-sawed timbers were produced. (3) Materials were then trucked to the construction site for each building. (4) After a concrete floor was in place there was little to do but swing a hammer because every piece was cut to fit a designated place. One crew nailed studding in place, another nailed up rafters, others sheeting and siding, others were on the roof. Finally, electrical, heating and plumbing crews took over.[63]

One observer commented, "Where there was a skeleton of a building yesterday, half a dozen new buildings stand today. Has Houdini come back? Well, you begin to wonder." The Army engineers'

Aerial view of the railroad siding and fuel tanks at the new Army Air Forces base in Sioux Falls. *Courtesy Doug Uthe.*

One of the hangars constructed at the base. *Courtesy Doug Uthe.*

staff was very demanding. One contractor remarked, "They crack the whip over us from the time we get the contract until the completion date." Another contractor observed that the slogan for the engineers should be, "Get it done, how you do it makes no difference, but get it done and quick."[64] Large progress clocks were set up at the sites of ten ongoing projects. The clocks showed the percentage of the project which had been completed. The clocks were accompanied by a slogan–"Close the gap and whip the Jap." Each contractor was allowed two weeks to bring a project up to schedule. Several of the Army engineers' cars were equipped with loudspeaker systems which were used to encourage the workers.[65]

In the September 7 issue of the *Argus Leader,* the editor paid tribute to Sioux Falls laborers: "As the army project is nearing conclusion, 'a significant factor is that the job has been accomplished without labor trouble. One reason, local labor units have been in charge. They sought to avoid trouble. They did not want outsiders to dictate their affairs and didn't want to exact exorbitant union fees.'"

Continual rains made it difficult for contractors to remain on schedule. Rain fell in Sioux Falls on twenty of the thirty-one days in May. Rainfall for the month totaled 7.18 inches, 2.9 inches ahead of the average precipitation for the month. The temperature for

The "checker board" roof of a new base hangar. *Courtesy Doug Uthe.*

May was 4.4 degrees below normal with a mean temperature of 54.3 degrees, the lowest for May since 1917. The excessive rainfall caused the Big Sioux River to overflow its banks northwest of the city.[66]

Severe thunderstorms struck the city on May 30-31. Gusts of wind reached seventy-two miles per hour. Field offices, partly finished barracks and mess halls were blown down. Several workmen were injured as the fierce wind filled the air with flying lumber. One construction foreman remarked that lumber and structure board were "scattered from Hell to breakfast." Roofs were blown off several warehouses, damaging the stock of "insulate" structural board.[67]

The first concrete for a warehouse was laid on May 19. The well-established, local concrete firm of Norlin and Stadem's Acme Concrete Company had the contract for three-fourths of the concrete work at the air base. They provided the concrete for the hospital, school, officers' quarters, and barracks. They poured concrete whether it rained or hailed. After one hail storm there were pockmarked slabs. The Acme firm had 299 men working on the project and the sixteen-hour day was the norm. Work continued during the night under lights as city crews had strung wires to the base.

Lil Norlin and Helge Stadem commented that often haste made waste as the Army engineers with their specifications in hand pushed all projects along. In putting down the floors for the school buildings and warehouses, Acme workmen discovered that the engineers had not measured right. When the buildings were placed on the concrete slabs, the slab protruded one foot outside of the walls. At one site, three loads of concrete were rejected and dumped by the engineers although the workers knew that it was perfectly good. Following specifications, engineers insisted that the slabs be 5.5 inches deep when 5 inches would have been adequate. The men kept their anger at the waste they observed to themselves. Paper by the ton was burned and a large tire collection was never used. Each barrack housed thirty-two men. They were poorly insulated as the walls consisted of wood covered with tar paper and lathe. There were two or three stoves in each barrack with a coal bin for two barracks.[68] There was a nearby barrack that contained latrine and shower facilities. The

During construction in April 1942, a violent wind storm temporarily delayed the building of barracks. *Center for Western Studies.*

soldiers, unfamiliar with soft coal stoves, piled on coats and blankets trying to keep warm during the winter months.[69] Ironically, barracks in South Carolina were well insulated.[70]

A brick structure housed the heating plant and provided steam heat for the classrooms, hospital and administration building. In early August, two theaters were completed, each one having seating capacity for 1,000 students. Three chapels, each one accommodating 300 people and equipped with movable altars and pulpits, were built. Any denomination could hold a service without delay. Room was provided for a choir. The chapels had finished paneled walls and hammered amber window glass.[71]

Much to the relief of the engineers and also the contractors, it was announced that the construction of the Army Air Corps Technical Training Command (AACTTC) School for radio training would be completed on June 28, well ahead of schedule. The engineers now were generous with their praise, proclaiming, "The morale of the men has been wonderful." One of the heavy equipment operators said, "I just wanted to tell you I am working as hard and as fast as I can on our air school job. It means a lot to me because I lost two sons on Bataan."[72]

In addition to Camblin and his staff, other key military administrative personnel and their staff had arrived in Sioux Falls in May and early June. On June 17, a twenty-truck convoy from Scott Field, Illinois, arrived in the city. The convoy carried the first of five squadrons—a total of 324 men—who would have administration of students when the school opened. The remainder of the squadrons arrived by rail. At the school's peak there would be nineteen squadrons. Upon their arrival, they were housed overnight in the Sioux Falls Coliseum. The early arrivals used the hangar at the Municipal Airport as their mess hall until the one on the base was completed.

Prior to the completion of the base hospital, military personnel used facilities at Sioux Valley Hospital. Marie Christopherson, who lived near the hospital, observed eight white-uniformed nurses walking abreast down the street. They were accompanied by Mrs. Anna Berdahl, an instructor in the hospital's school of nursing. She stopped to talk with Mrs. Christopherson and reported that the young women were student nurses. She went on to say that "The soldier boys are using our classrooms, so we are having class at my house."

REVEILLE FOR SIOUX FALLS

At an open house on the first floor of the hospital, C. M. Austin, the hospital's superintendent, showed guests several wards that had been hurriedly furnished for men from the air base. There were several enlisted men who were hospitalized with colds. Regarding these new patients, Austin said, "Funny thing is the boys are dismissed one day and the next day they are back to call on the nurses."[73]

As of June 23, military police could be seen patrolling the downtown area. On July 2, the first trainload of students arrived, and four days later, Monday, July 6, classes were underway. Camblin had been reassigned to Jefferson Barracks, Missouri. Before his departure, he declared that the average Sioux Falls citizen has not been able to comprehend what is going to hit the city when the mass of men arrive.[74] His replacement was Colonel N. L. Cote, from Scott Field, Illinois.[75]

Crowded troop trains began to arrive regularly at the Chicago, Milwaukee & St. Paul Depot in Sioux Falls. As they got off of the train, the incoming GIs were met by one of the base chaplains. He provided a cheerful, revealing message of the life they might expect at the Sioux Falls Army Technical School. The new arrivals were first directed to the recovery and shipping area where they were inspected for contagious diseases and assigned temporary living quarters. Their records were collected and checked according to classification, finance, personal affairs, service records and training. The entire processing of incoming students took two to three days in the following order: (1) Received inoculations and vaccinations; (2) Received means of identification; (3) Checking and stamping of dog tags; photographed and picture placed on a pass; (4) Clothing inspection: shortages were filled. If clothing order was over-issued, said clothing was reclaimed; (5) Received training cards, pay codes, student assignments and then were moved to their school section and barracks.[76]

Phillips Avenue had a new look as men in khaki-colored uniforms thronged the sidewalks. Civic leaders sat back and rejoiced as their hopes and plans for a rejuvenated economy came to fruition. The new base was dedicated on August 22, 1942. Senator Chan Gurney arranged for six planes to circle the base and land.[77] Seated on the reviewing stand were 128 officers and 40 civilians. General Frederick L. Martin, after reviewing 1,000 troops, gave a brief speech. He was in charge of the 2nd District of the AAF Technical Training Command,

Phillips Avenue, downtown Sioux Falls, summer 1942. *Center for Western Studies.*

headquartered in St. Louis. Seating was provided for 10,000 people.[78] The quiet city was about to undergo great change as the Army Air Corps Technical Training School made its indelible economic and social impact upon the community. The growth and change would continue after World War II.

# Chapter 2

## PROSPERITY AND PROBLEMS

*Sioux Falls has taken the soldier right into the
family circle. I went to church this morning
and upon leaving was invited by three different
families into their homes for the day.
– An ATS soldier from Elyria, Ohio.*

In the spring of 1943, J. A. Bailey, a reporter from the *Aberdeen American News*, visited Sioux Falls. He commented at length on the overwhelming presence of the military. There were uniforms galore on Phillips Avenue. Planes droned overhead at frequent intervals. Women in uniform chauffeured officers about the city. Jeeps and army trucks claimed the right-of-way. He wrote, "Sioux Falls offers the most realistic picture I have seen of South Dakota at war, and when the fracas ends, outside of a few minor headaches and maybe a shorter stride, she'll keep on the road ahead." After touring the Army Technical School, Bailey commented, "And on top of all that, Sioux Falls is as proud of the Army Post as a hen is of a brand new consignment of chicks."[1] In addition to changing the city's physical and social character, the school played a pivotal role in rejuvenating the city's economy.

A different view was expressed by the editor of the *Vermillion Republican* who spent a weekend in Sioux Falls. He said, "But a weekend spent in Sioux Falls confirms us in the belief that those communities are most fortunate who do not have to endure the discomforts of speeding up business of all kinds to take care of a vast increase in normal population. It is difficult to secure hotel accommodations in Sioux Falls. It is equally difficult to secure apartments or living quarters of any kind. Eating at restaurants is expensive and the portions served are a mere aggravation to a hungry man. Stores, theaters, and streets are crowded. Among the thousands of soldiers on the street, we did not see a single instance of intoxication or misconduct of any kind. The boys seem to be tending strictly to their own business and not bothering anyone. Undoubtedly, some lines of business are making plenty of money out of the proximity of a large army camp."[2]

## THE NEW PROSPERITY

Soldiers who were off-duty for the weekend began arriving in downtown Sioux Falls shortly after the noon hour on Friday. It became nearly impossible at the air base gates to get a taxi without waiting twenty minutes to two hours. Cab drivers reveled in their newfound business. One man remarked that cab drivers were making $70 a week with one day off. In the past, $18 a day made them happy. By nightfall, the streets and sidewalks were filled with young men in khaki uniforms.

The Army Technical School (ATS) became a lifesaver for the city's amusement business. Weekend crowds were jammed three deep in the bars with limited standing room. For the GIs, dancing was the preferred form of entertainment. The Arkota Ballroom usually featured the swing band sounds of Louis Armstrong, Duke Ellington, the more subdued sounds of Lawrence Welk and popular area bands. Night club owners had a shortage of help, finding it difficult to find qualified musicians. Although the movie theaters at the base played 95 percent of new moving picture shows ahead of downtown theaters, young servicemen waited in line with their friends or girlfriends, if they were lucky enough to have a date, to see a movie at the Egyptian, Hollywood, State, Orpheum or Time theaters. Restaurants in 1942 had a 50 percent increase in business over levels of 1941. People were buying steak, not hamburger. The young GIs enjoyed snacks at the Palace of Sweets or the Chocolate Shop on Phillips Avenue. There were a large number of out-of-town guests in the city each weekend. Advance reservations were required at hotels and soldiers were asked to double-up, sleeping three to four men per room on cots or twin beds. Despite the restrictions on off-sale liquor to servicemen between 5:00 and 10:00 P.M., people involved in liquor sales experienced their best business in history.

The city's police chief, J. W. Galvin, and the military police (MPs) shared the burden of keeping carefree soldiers under control. The MPs had their headquarters in the police department and they worked closely with the police. MPs rode with the police part of the time.[3]

The Army Technical School provided over 1,800 civilian jobs and vastly increased the demand for workers in restaurants and entertainment establishments. Local women also stepped into vacancies left by men who departed for military service. Industries such as John Morrell and Co. and Sioux Steel, previously dominated by male laborers, were now permeated by women in coveralls.[4]

The construction of the Army Technical School and the arrival of thousands of servicemen in the city contributed significantly to a decline in the federal government's aid programs that had been established during the 1930s. Since the inception of the Works Progress Administration (WPA) in 1935, approximately $5 million had been expended in Minnehaha County. At the peak of the Great Depression, the WPA employed slightly over 3,000 men in the county. By 1939, work rolls contained the names of 1,199 men. In May 1942, the number was 88. With the great demand for war material and millions of men now serving in the armed forces, it was announced that, nationally, the WPA would be liquidated on February 1, 1943. In September 1942, only one crew of fourteen men was involved in a construction project. They were building a retaining wall at Emerson School.[5] The state administrator of the WPA, M. A. Kennedy, announced that the South Dakota WPA office would be closed permanently as of April 3, 1943.[6]

In mid-September 1942, the county's direct relief fund had been reduced $2,378 from August 1941. The total for August 1941 was $8,658.82. In August 1942, the total was $6,280.67. The total case load in August 1941 was 586. It was reduced to 444 in August 1942. No employable workers were included in the August total. Most of the relief expenditure went to families without working fathers. Employment remained plentiful. Men who were released after completion of the ATS had found jobs elsewhere, accompanying contractors to other sites of construction.[7]

The growing prosperity of Sioux Falls led to an unprecedented increase in bank clearings. These indicated the amount of money in circulation and were considered the most accurate indicator of prosperity. The total bank clearings were $105,237,397.46 in 1941 and $136,345,024.88 in 1942, an increase of $31,107,627.42. This significant gain was due not only to the advent of the Army Technical

School, but also to the area's bumper crop and improved prices for agricultural products.[8]

## MONTHLY BANK CLEARINGS 1941-1942

|  | 1941 | 1942 |
| --- | --- | --- |
| January | $7,347,778.89 | 11,445,088.49 |
| February | 6,511,939.32 | 9,324,379.00 |
| March | 7,290,199.25 | 9,984,335.05 |
| April | 8,425,834.97 | 9,942,593.15 |
| May | 9,309,486.57 | 10,233,067.31 |
| June | 8,804,701.16 | 12,503,685.28 |
| July | 9,601,548.76 | 13,119,641.28 |
| August | 8,301,593.86 | 10,534,901.72 |
| September | 9,360,655.91 | 11,086,793.89 |
| October | 9,714,313.94 | 11,127,197.19 |
| November | 9,675,841.98 | 11,060,268.77 |
| December | 10,892,506.85 | 13,983,073.75[9] |

## HOSPITALITY

*Twas the night before Christmas*
*And throughout the Post*
*The soldiers were musing*
*On what they'd like most.*
*'Twas the night before Christmas*
*The eve of good cheer*
*But his family kept thinking*
*If Eddie were here.*
*Eddie feasted on turkey*
*With the Larsons in town*
*While his folks back in Brooklyn*
*Fed a sailor named Brown.*
*- Polar Tech, December 17, 1943*

As thousands of GIs descended upon Sioux Falls, civic leaders called upon the city's residents to treat the incoming military personnel as they would want their own sons and brothers, now in the service elsewhere, to be treated. The Chamber of Commerce urged residents to invite one or two young servicemen to Sunday dinner. Paul

Meyers, secretary for the Chamber of Commerce, noted the appeal of a home-cooked meal to soldiers.[10] There was an overwhelming response of local residents to the Chamber's suggestion. One month after the first detachment of troops arrived, the Servicemen's Center had 400 homes on a list of people who would entertain soldiers for Sunday dinner. Men from the ATS who attended local churches were invariably invited to dinner after worship services. Sometimes the dinner was preceded by a drive around the city. Families sacrificed their food ration coupons to host the soldiers. The women of West Nidaros Church brought 1,500 cookies and doughnuts to the Service Information Center.[11] In addition to a home-cooked meal, homesick boys loved to hear the wife play the piano and to chat about things in the civilian world.[12] The soldiers reciprocated in a variety of ways. They mowed lawns, ran locker rooms at the YMCA during rush hours and served as organists and soloists at local churches. At Augustana Lutheran Church, graduates of musical conservatories served as leaders of the music program while stationed at the ATS.

The record was set by the Sherman Iverson family, who owned a 160-acre farm on the south edge of the city. Between 1942 and 1944, they invited fifteen to thirty soldiers for Sunday dinner once a week. It was estimated that approximately 2,000 men had spent a day at the farm. After the meal, the GIs did KP duty in the kitchen, adjourned to the parlor to sing or, if the weather was nice, rode horses, went for a swim, drove the tractor or asked if they could help with the chores.[13] On Thanksgiving Day, 1942, more than 150 invitations were issued by local families asking soldiers to share dinner with them. Increased demands for certain food products caused the editor of *Polar Tech* in late March 1943 to ask soldiers not to accept many dinner invitations. Several foodstuffs were being added to the rationed list. Meat, butter, cheese, fats and oils joined coffee, sugar and canned goods as the products that could only be purchased with ration coupons. The editor wrote, "For civilian families an extra guest may mean that the family will have to do without essential food items for a short time." He realized that his fellow GIs enjoyed the hospitality but, he declared, "others should not suffer for it."[14] While discouraging the acceptance of dinner invitations, he urged the men to drop in at the host home in the afternoon or later in the evening.

## PHEASANT HUNTING

The *Argus Leader* urged the state Game and Fish Department to grant the students at the ATS hunting privileges while stationed in South Dakota. The request was approved and local hunters began to host ATS personnel on pheasant hunts beginning on September 20, 1942. The men, having proved they knew the state's game laws, could secure a non-resident license for $1.00 at the base. They could check-out a shotgun for twenty-four hours and secure fifty rounds of ammunition per week.[15] Local hunters contributed much of the game they shot to the base kitchen, and the birds were used as the main entrée for dinner at the ATS.[16] The local Izaak Walton League sponsored a "Take a Soldier Hunting Campaign" in October 1944. Dozens of local citizens signed up to take GIs with them on hunting excursions on a Sunday in October when most of the soldiers were off-duty. The pheasants were plentiful and one group got their limit in little more than two hours. The hunters stated they could have killed more than fifty birds if they had not adhered to the legal limit.[17] If the GIs wanted to hunt migratory water fowl, they had to purchase a duck stamp.

## DANCING AT THE USO

Young women from the region were recruited to help entertain the GIs at picnics, parties and dances. Mrs. E. B. Goodrich enlisted the aid of approximately 350 "personality girls" to be on the list of entertainers. Each girl underwent a personal interview. Mrs. Goodrich said, "We want girls from every walk of life, just as long as their character is irreproachable." Their behavior would be strictly regulated—and the young women were to wear sweaters and skirts even at picnics.[18]

When dances were held at the base, girls were provided by three social organizations. The invited girls were issued a small cardboard tag which had to be worn to gain admittance to the military installation.[19] Women attending dances at the ATS belonged to the Military Misses, the Khaki Pals, or to the largest group, the Techettes.[20] The Techettes, who were organized and even had elected officers, celebrated their second anniversary in August 1944. Later,

Lucky GIs meet the Techettes, a group of young ladies from Sioux Falls organized by Mrs. E. R. Goodrich (center) to provide companionship. *Center for Western Studies.*

they had large yellow pins with name tags. From a roster of over 250 women, an average of 135 girls attended at least one dance per week, providing partners for the soldiers.[21] They also participated in the annual Sadie Hawkins dance at the Sioux Falls Coliseum. All of the girls were asked to dress like Daisy Mae, with short skirts and dazzling blouses.[22]

Vincent Galvin, Director of the United Services Organizations (USO) Center at 11th and Main Avenue, reported that dancing was the most popular form of entertainment for the soldiers. He gave much credit to the "Victory Belles" or junior hostesses. They assured the success of dancing parties.[23] Vincent Galvin opened the doors of the USO at 11th and Main in November 1942. He proved efficient and remained on the job to the war's end. He had worked at a local clothing store, Weatherwax's, for seventeen years. Prior to that, he was Director of Athletics at Columbus College, coaching basketball, football and track teams.[24]

Service centers provided a more organized type of hospitality for the GIs stationed at the ATS. The first center was established in the basement of First Lutheran Church in July 1942 as prospective radio operators occupied the barracks at the newly constructed Army Technical School. First Lutheran was joined in this endeavor, subsidized by the National Lutheran Council Service Commission, by East Side and Augustana Lutheran congregations. The center was designed to meet the soldiers' spiritual and social needs.

Not until September 1942 did the USO make its presence felt in Sioux Falls. The USO was founded on February 4, 1941, by six national agencies prominent in the religious and welfare fields. It was a nonprofit agency dedicated to providing food, entertainment and shelter for U.S. servicemen wherever they were stationed.[25]

Until September, a volunteer committee, chaired by businessman Joseph L. Floyd, had taken charge of defense recreation and provided several services for the newly arrived GIs.[26] On September 1, 1942, the Minnesota Avenue USO was dedicated. It was housed in the YMCA, taking up one-half of the ground floor of the building. The site was remodeled to include a large lounge, social room and a separate reading room. It was to be jointly operated by the YMCA and the Jewish Welfare Board. J. M. Street was the director. On October 22, all the facilities at the "Y" were offered, free of charge, to servicemen. All men in uniform were extended full membership.[27] This USO remained open until January 15, 1946, to accommodate a skeleton crew of 1,055 personnel who remained at the base to process the discharge of returning Army airmen.[28]

By late October, residents of Sioux Falls began to ask when a stand-alone USO would be established. They had been told in April that a USO would be on the job when the Army base opened. People had not expected a delay as they had given freely and generously the funds necessary for a USO.[29]

The long awaited authorization from the bureaucrats in the nation's capital arrived a few days later. The site for the USO had already been determined. The vacated Borgen Chevrolet garage at Main Avenue and 11th Street had become available when the area office of the U.S. Army Engineers was moved to the Army Technical School. Harold T. Spitznagel, a local architect, who had designed military housing at the Army air base, played a key role in the remodeling of the former garage into a modern downtown recreation center. A new entrance was constructed; a lounge, activity rooms and a floor for dancing were the first major improvements to what became known as the Main Avenue USO.[30] The costs for the first remodeling project, estimated at $10,000, were financed by the Federal Security Agency. The new center was operated by the National Catholic Community Service (NCCS) and the YMCA. The Main Avenue USO, which opened on November 10, 1942, continued to be a work in progress. In early May 1943, the national USO granted an additional $33,000 for further remodeling of the center.[31]

The center ultimately had a large auditorium for dancing with a stage at one end. There was a game room, music room, a crafts room equipped with modern tools, a lunch counter, four special club rooms, a sound-proof recording room, a large lounge, a check room for clothing, offices and a small café, Louis' Eat Shoppe, that served coffee and sandwiches. There were dressing rooms adjoining the stage. Also available for the GIs was a long-distance telephone center with eight booths, a piano, radio and new motion picture equipment.[32] The center was open from 10:00 A.M. until midnight.

Acknowledging the soldiers' penchant for dancing, Galvin announced that there would be regular Saturday night dances. The local Victory Belles were available as partners, and chaperones were on duty at all times.[33] Dance instruction was available for men who had not mastered the two-step or waltz. The latest movies were shown and very often men could be seen gathered around the piano and harmonizing.[34]

Just south of the USO was a tent used by the servicemen for playing cards or writing letters on hot summer days or evenings. The tent was destroyed by a fire on August 30, 1943.[35] Like the Minnesota Avenue USO, the Main Avenue facility assisted GIs in making contact with local citizens regarding invitations to dinner. Christmas Day was the busiest day of the year for USO personnel. On December 25, 1942, the two USOs handled more than 1,260 invitations to dinner. Over 6,000 men were entertained at the Main Avenue club with the ATS orchestra providing dance music.[36]

Louis R. Hurwitz, president of the USO council, and his committee, began a summer-long program of weekly USO picnics in the parks for the GIs and the WACs. Various societies and local clubs provided the entertainment and food for these gatherings.[37] By February 1944, over 800,000 men had visited one or both of the centers with the average attendance totaling more than 2,000 visitors per day.[38]

A third USO opened in the fall of 1942. Plans were approved and funds appropriated for an African-American USO in the Margulies Building at 115 North Dakota Avenue. It was formally dedicated on February 1, 1943.[39] Black soldiers and their wives operated the club. It accommodated the all-black 85th Aviation Squadron and the 929th Quartermaster Platoon. These units were under the command of Captain J.E. Shannon.[40]

Several other service centers were established to accommodate the troops. The 40-8 Servicemen's Club opened in January 1943 at 214 West 10th Street. Past active members of the American Legion welcomed not only the soldiers but also their wives or girlfriends.[41] GIs also relied on the Servicemen's Information Center at 216 North Phillips Avenue.[42] When the ATS was transformed into a redeployment base following the Allied victory in Europe, a Jewish Service Center opened at 610 South Dakota Avenue near 14th Street in the basement of the Sons of Israel Synagogue. The center, which opened on July 31, 1945, was sponsored by B'nai B'rith and local Jewish citizens. Entertainment consisted of social gatherings accompanied by cool drinks and delicacies.[43]

Officers had their club on the base while the NCOs (non-commissioned officers) had a club off-base in the Cataract Hotel. Dances were held at the hotel on Thursday, Saturday and Sunday evenings. Twice a month, on Tuesday evening, dancing in the main ballroom followed a buffet dinner. A stag buffet was held once a month. The NCO's club included comfortable lounges and nooks for reading newspapers and magazines.[44]

For many women whose boyfriends were abroad, soldiers became substitute dates. Although they missed the local boys, they had a great deal of fun at dances, roasting ears of corn at bonfires at Wall Lake, sharing food at the Chocolate Shop on Phillips Avenue, which advertised itself as "Adventures in Good Eating," the Palace of Sweets and the Town 'n Country Café on West 12th Street. There were five movie theaters in the city where soldiers could take their local dates.[45] One local woman, who met her future husband at the Chocolate Shop, best described the dating scene with these words:

"With most of the local boys in the service somewhere else, [Sioux Falls] was a haven for a lot of girls because of the thousands of men stationed at the base."[46]

A large number of the young women who served as hostesses at dances and other planned functions married men from the Army Technical School. By August 1942, two months after the first soldiers arrived in Sioux Falls, a wedding boom had begun. By the end of the year, 837 wedding licenses had been issued compared with 576 in 1941, a 45 percent increase.[47] In December 1942, a record was set as 144 licenses were issued by the Clerk of Courts. Ninety percent of licenses were obtained by soldiers. Sixty percent of the applicants left the Clerk of Court's office to go directly to the Base Chaplain, a Catholic priest, county judge or a Protestant pastor in that order. The remaining 40 percent were married within ten days after their licenses were issued.

A wedding license cost $1.25, and health certificates were required.[48] The court used the help of the ATS Red Cross station to certify the age of the GI applicants. The average age of the bridegroom was twenty three and twenty for the bride. Many of the brides were local, living within an eighty mile radius of Sioux Falls.[49] Marie Christopherson, in her column "Driftwood," frequently published in the *Argus Leader,* commented that many of the young women often married men whom they had met only recently. She warned young women that a few weeks' or a few months' acquaintance does not always reveal an individual's character. The young women should be checking on their suitor's background.[50]

GIs from Illinois, New York, Pennsylvania and California led the list of soldiers marrying local girls. By mid-July 1944, at least 355 soldiers had taken local women as their brides.[51] After the war, several of the married couples returned to Sioux Falls and the adjacent area to establish residence and raise their children. They moved to Sioux Falls because their wives wanted to return to their roots and the men had found Sioux Falls to be a friendly, welcoming and hospitable community.

Some of the men had misgivings when they first learned they would be assigned to the Sioux Falls Army Technical School. Francis Mainolfi thought everybody would be riding horses in Sioux Falls, which he assumed was a real cow town. Harold Wingler thought he would be stationed at the end of the world when he received his orders to report to the ATS.[52] Private Harry Anderson, who had been stationed at Scott Field, Illinois, wrote that "We were rather skeptical about our new assignment, having heard a lot of stories about the Indians here and so forth. Upon arrival in Sioux Falls, we certainly found things a lot different."[53]

Harold Wingler soon changed his mind. He later commented that "Lots of towns hated GIs. But this was the nicest Army town any GI ever hit. The people treated the soldiers as one of the family."[54] The second class to graduate from the ATS addressed the people of Sioux Falls with the following statement in the *Argus Leader*: "You have treated us not just as your guests, but as though we were your sons, brothers, and close friends home on leave from the service."[55] A mother from Alden, Pennsylvania, wrote to the *Argus Leader:* ". . . I am deeply grateful for the kindness not only to my son but to all the boys who were so far from home. If you know of any boy stationed in or near Philadelphia whose home is in Sioux Falls, I would like to have his address here."[56] A mother in Virginia received the following statement from her son stationed at the ATS: "This is a swell town, Mom. All the girls, men and women, even boys will talk to a fellow. I didn't know there was a town like this in the USA. I sure would like to live here when this is all over."[57]

## A NIGHT WITH VENUS ISN'T WORTH A LIFETIME OF MERCURY

There were troubles, however, in this prairie community on the banks of the Big Sioux River. Prior to 1942, the police knew that prostitution existed in Sioux Falls but they tolerated it as long as the prostitutes stayed in their residences and carried out their trade in their rooms. If they engaged in liaisons on the streets, the police would bring them in and run them through the courts.[58] The offenders either spent time in jail or were told to leave the city. As thousands of laborers gathered to construct the new military facility in the spring of 1942, several women, some of whom were diseased, had come to Sioux Falls.[59]

Dr. Emil G. Erickson, health officer in Sioux Falls, declared his "department is working 100% with Army authorities in meeting the evils of infection arising from prostitution." Sioux Falls maintained a public venereal disease clinic. Efforts were made to keep per capita disease rates at a low level.  The city required trailer camps to be licensed in an effort to keep a check on such camps and other possible sources of infectious disease.[60]

In November 1942, community leaders in Sioux Falls met with Colonel Cote and medical officers from the ATS to discuss the growing problem of venereal disease.[61]  By this time, officers at the Army Technical School were often asked to speak at the Rotary and Kiwanis clubs.  Captain E.E. Seiler stunned his audience when he strongly recommended that there be a clean-up campaign to eliminate prostitution in the city and in adjacent areas.  Health officers at the school were finding that many soldiers had been diagnosed with venereal disease.[62]  Seiler recommended eliminating several "shady" night spots in the city's vicinity and urged parents to be aware of where their daughters were in the evening. He asked parents not to hesitate to act as chaperones.  The editor of the *Argus Leader* commented that Seiler's recommendations should not be ignored.[63]

In early December, Lieutenant Joseph Hirsh, Venereal Disease Control Officer at the ATS, spoke to a council of social agencies.  He outlined a five-point program for controlling venereal disease:

1. Establish a detention hospital for infected women, isolate them and treat them effectively.

2. Enforce a local curfew ordinance to get early teenage youngsters off the streets.  Many of them were walking Main and Phillips avenues until 1:00 or 2:00 A.M. engaged in "window shopping," or begging to be picked up.  One source described them as "throwing themselves at soldiers."  Many of these girls were willing to have sex with soldiers for small favors such as being taken to a movie or treated to a snack at the Chocolate Shop or the Palace of Sweets.  Among soldiers, they were known as "charity girls."  Hirsh indicated that they had replaced commercial prostitutes.

3. The city fathers were urged to create a better mass recreational program for teenagers to get them off of the streets.

4. A sound sex hygiene program should be established in the public school system for older teenagers.

5. Hirsh strongly recommended that additional personnel and appropriations were needed for health and police services.[64]

What occurred in Sioux Falls was not unique. In the United States, in 1943, the number of teenage girls arrested increased by 68 percent over the previous year. Nationally, they were known as V (for victory) girls. The girls, some barely thirteen, were known for their Sloppy Joe sweaters, hair ribbons, anklets or bobby socks, saddle shoes and heavily made-up faces. Many of them had a misguided sense of patriotism believing that they were contributing to the war effort by giving themselves to a man in uniform. They were "khaki-wacky," willing to indulge in promiscuity because of the glamour of the uniform.[65]

The City Commission approved the most drastic dance regulations ever enacted in Sioux Falls. It reclassified and redefined a public dance. The ordinance stipulated that there must be adequate illumination of the grounds and the dance floor. There was to be no immodest, suggestive, lewd or immoral dancing. There would be no dancing on Sunday although dancing was permitted until 2:00 A.M. on Sunday morning.[66]

In late January 1943, the City Commission passed another ordinance authorizing the employment of special police matrons with police powers. The goal was to extend the police department's drive against vice and delinquency. The matrons were to be employed in hotels and amusement centers with the operators of said businesses paying the matron's wages.[67]

Several commercial prostitutes, who had remained in the city, were arrested in the last days of January. The editor of the *Argus Leader* commented that "They and their kind will soon learn that Sioux Falls is not healthy for them." Teenagers discovered that violations of the curfew would not be tolerated. Four police women were put on duty in plain clothes to supplement the matrons in hotels and amusement places. Consideration was given to the need for detention hospital facilities because of the lack of hospital space in the city.[68]

During the early morning hours of March 7, 1943, local, county, and city police joined with the military police from the ATS in launching a sweep of establishments selling alcoholic beverages as far away as Luverne, Minnesota. They sought violators of the ATS rule that soldiers could not purchase beer or liquor after 11:00 P.M. Both bootleggers and prostitutes were arrested in these raids.[69]  In an effort to curb undesirables from registering at hotels, all unescorted female guests of ATS personnel were required to have an identification card issued by the Provost Marshal at the Air Base when registering.  Single women who were not associated with the ATS did not need cards but they would be closely watched by police matrons.

The editor of *Polar Tech*, writing in the December 10, 1943, issue, commented that "A soldier with venereal disease is wounded if he ends up in the hospital.  He must receive costly and painful treatment. Until he returns to duty some one else has to take his job.  He forfeits his pay, blackens the eye of himself, family and his organization. All the time that he loses must be made-up—the duration plus six months plus the loss of time. City authorities are doing a good job of keeping the city clean but there are girls who manage to stay on the loose before getting caught. *'Don't be one of the careless soldiers who get burned.  A night with Venus isn't worth a lifetime of mercury.'*"[70]

Lieutenant Hirsch, speaking at the local Rotary Club, said the effects of VD would be felt long after the war and when the Army Technical School was just a memory.  He stated that almost 50 percent of the men infected with gonorrhea had liaisons with girls sixteen to twenty years of age. He believed these young women were desperately in need of medical, social and educational assistance.  Hirsch concluded his remarks by stating, "You can't win this year's health battles with last year's appropriation, personnel and strategy."[71]

An isolation and detention center for young women having gonorrhea finally opened on May 1, 1943.  Girls identified as a source of infection would be confined at the center for observation and, if needed, treatment.  Over a period of five months, Mayor C. M. Whitfield had labored to seek funds for a place to house the "charity girls."  The detention center, located in an apartment building near city hall, became a reality through cooperation with the State Board of Health. The detention center had a full-time matron and manager.[72] The Board provided financial assistance that was matched by funds obtained from the U.S. Public Health Service.  Dr. F. H. Rediwill, City Health Director said, "The importance of ample control of venereal diseases cannot be overemphasized at this time.  With the approach of the summer season, however, the problem can be expected to increase."[73]

The venereal disease records for the Army Technical School were classified and never published. The army limited its public commentary on the disease after 1943, but one can assume that there was a lower incidence of gonorrhea during the remainder of World War II.

## THE HOUSING CRISIS AND GREEDY LANDLORDS

Inadequate housing also created problems throughout the war. Many of the soldiers and civilian employees arriving at the Army Technical School were married and had families. By mid-July 1942, there was a keen demand for houses and apartments, furnished and unfurnished. Real estate agents and the office of the Federal Housing Administration (FHA) were swamped with inquiries. The base's newspaper, *Polar Tech,* warned GIs to keep their families out of Sioux Falls if their loved ones were to have a roof over their heads. As of September 6, almost all of the housing space in the city had been exhausted. Some sleeping rooms for men were still available.[74]

The FHA solicited applications for remodeling, hoping to provide additional housing. Interested parties could apply for $100 worth of critical materials. When multiplied by the number of additional rooms to be provided, a large home could possibly have $800 available to purchase essential materials.[75]

After a quick survey of the city and learning that 2,400 more units would be required, the Chamber of Commerce requested a defense housing designation.[76] Within three weeks, N. I. Blegen, the state FHA manager, received notice that Sioux Falls had been designated a war housing area. Blegen indicated that the designation did "not mean that anyone can go ahead and build a house as they would under normal times." Houses or units that would be built had to be sold or rented only to war workers. The new dwellings would be divided into assorted rent brackets. Blegen indicated that the city's first quota was 150 units.[77] Optimism turned to gloom when the Victory Housing Project of 150 homes was delayed because of material shortages and bureaucratic "red tape."[78] Despite pleas from the Chamber of Commerce, local contractors were reluctant to build homes under the government's rubric. Six weeks had passed and local builders had applied to construct only twenty of the proposed 150 new residences. The federal housing coordinator's office in Chicago issued an ultimatum. If local private builders and private capital did not take up the priorities and build, the housing administration would send in outside contractors and private capital to provide the needed housing.[79]

The government quickly contracted with the Peder Mickelsen firm in Minneapolis to build seventy housing units in Sioux Falls. They were to be constructed between 12th and 15th streets on Glendale and Hawthorne avenues. The contractor promised to have some of the houses ready for occupancy in sixty to ninety days. The four-room houses, constructed of brick and tile, would compare favorably with a $5,000 house before the war. The rentals would be handled through the War Housing Agency and would be leased only to persons engaged in war work or moving to the city for necessary reasons.[80]

Much of the new construction took place between 6th and 18th streets west of Minnesota Avenue. There were two exceptions: several duplexes in the 26th block of South Duluth Avenue and a few houses southeast of McKennan Hospital. The *Argus Leader* was critical of the construction of small homes, calling them sheep-shed structures with forty-foot wide frontage. The newspaper said that there was plenty of room for fifty-foot lots.[81] Much of the new construction had to be offered to war workers for sixty days after construction was completed.

Many homeowners had taken up the FHA's offer to use the $100 per unit to remodel their homes. Within two months, between 125 and 140 additional rooms and units had been created by splitting houses into duplexes, dividing rooms into apartments and by partitioning large spaces into smaller rooms.[82]

At the end of September 1942, the demand for rental properties was greater than the supply. Landlords realized they had a seller's market working in their favor and they quickly took advantage of it. A potential tenant, desperately in need of a place to live, was not about to quibble over the price he was asked to pay. He needed a home or apartment. The majority of landlords were reasonable; they had made fair adjustments in rental rates. There were other landlords, however, who took advantage of the prevailing situation. They raised prices as high as the traffic would bear and it appeared the traffic could stand quite a bit.

Want ads in the *Argus Leader* that indicated a few apartments and housekeeping rooms for rent usually cited no prices. Rents were out of control by August 15, 1942, and irate tenants began to deluge the Chamber of Commerce with letters and calls denouncing landlords and filing complaints. One tenant wrote, "What's this about a rent ceiling? I read in the paper that there's supposed to be one, yet my landlord says he wants 10 bucks more a month or I'll have to get out." The Chamber of Commerce advised victims of obvious rent gouging practices to do the following: (1) Write two checks when paying your monthly rent, one for the regular rent and other for the increase, insisting on two receipts. (2) Write a letter to the Chamber setting forth the circumstance. (3) Sit tight and wait.[83]

On March 1, 1942, rents had been frozen and Sioux Falls had been designated a rent-control city. On June 3, there began a sixty-day waiting period to see if landlords would comply voluntarily. The waiting period expired August 3 and, immediately, rental fees had risen sharply. Landlords argued vigorously that March 1 had not been a fair date as rental rates were in decline at that time. The local press indicated that landlords were indulging in sheer burglary as far as apartment house rentals were concerned.[84]

The federal government delayed establishing an Office of Price Administration (OPA) in Sioux Falls. An OPA representative, after visiting the city, indicated an office would be set up shortly. Finally, on October 11, 1942, the government announced that rates would be fixed at March 1 levels and the OPA issued an order freezing rents on November 1. It was announced on October 29 that Louis N. Crill, former Minnehaha County States Attorney (1933-1937), would be the rent control officer for the Sioux Falls area. He would administer rent control regulations in a five county area as of November 1. On that date, renters were advised to pay no more and landlords were ordered not to collect rents higher than were charged for the same quarters and services as of March 1. The order covered all types of housing accommodations except hotels and rooming houses. Tenants were informed that they could not be evicted for refusal to pay a rent higher than the legal rate. If they were threatened with eviction, they were to call Crill's office immediately.[85]

Several of the landlords found it difficult to accept the government's mandate. Some of them reluctantly filled out questionnaires and registration forms that provided information about their property. By December 21, 1942, Crill's office had received 11,400 registrations. His office sent all tenants copies of the registration form listing the March 1 rental rates and the legal maximum of said rates. Tenants were told that if a landlord collected more than the maximum legal rent, they could sue for triple damages or $50, whichever was higher.[86] Landlords who violated the March 1 rate were subject to a maximum fine of $5,000, one year in jail, or both. They could increase rents beyond the March 1 level if a major improvement had been made in the property or the accommodations had been changed from unfurnished to furnished.[87] The editor of *Polar Tech* advised soldiers whose families were living in off-base rental housing to procure a receipt or pay by check so that a record would be available for possible future adjustments.[88] Weekly rentals and services that Crill considered as fair and maximums were as follows:

| Class 1 | Single Room | $2.00 | Double Room | $3.00 |
| Class 2 | Single Room | $2.00 | Double Room | $4.00 |
| Class 3 | Single Room | $2.00 | Double Room | $6.00 |

The single room must have a bed, a place to hang clothes, mirror, chest of drawers and one or more chairs. The landlord would pay for all the utilities.

On January 1, 1943, architect Harold Spitznagel was appointed manager of the local housing center. His immediate task was to ask homeowners to lease their homes to the government to accommodate workers at the base and soldiers whose families had followed them to Sioux Falls. Spitznagel sought houses that could be converted into extra family dwellings and where zoning restrictions would permit construction. The government would remodel the house if the plans were approved by the homeowner. The homeowner received an adequate annual payment with payments three months in advance. The homeowner could retain one unit in the remodeled house for himself and his family by paying a monthly rental fee to the government. The government would pay all taxes, assessments, insurance, interest and payment on principal of the mortgage, if any, and pay current operating expenses in addition to keeping up the property for the duration of the lease.

Within three weeks, 105 homeowners had applied to lease their homes. Many were good properties that made excellent conversions. Preference was to be given to creating multi-family dwellings. The government set a conversion quota for the city.

In early February, 1943, Spitznagel was asked to design facilities for the military in Rapid City, Edgemont and Custer. He was also charged with the supervision of a war housing project in Rapid City. As he left Sioux Falls, 184 applications for government financed conversions had been received. It was announced that there was a great need for sleeping rooms as well as apartments.[89] In early June, 1943, Carl N. Forslund succeeded Spitznagel as director of the Sioux Falls War Housing Center.[90]

As the citizens of Sioux Falls welcomed the New Year in 1943, city accommodations were bursting at the seam. Living quarters for 500 instructors and other war workers were needed within the next six months. Three approaches to meeting the crisis were advanced: (1) Construct small, permanent dwellings, which were already underway. (2) Convert existing units to accommodate more families. (3) Construct temporary housing facilities at government expense.[91] The local press favored the second option.

Landlords continued to find it difficult to come to terms with the rental fee set by the federal government. They felt they were unfairly treated by being forced to abide by the March 1, 1942, limitation. They argued that they were the victims of administration by the OPA, that the OPA was keeping rents down but nothing else. They said they were paying 100 percent more to have coal hauled compared with pre-war costs. One landlord wrote, "Depression rents won't pay for worn rugs and furniture due to lack of getting vacuum sweepers to keep them clean." Landlords believed that there would be a surplus of housing after the war and they would suffer.[92]

Using a charter dating back to October 12, 1934, the landlords met on March 5, 1943, to organize an association: sixty-eight landlords indicated a desire to join the association. Within ten days they claimed a membership of 100. Membership fees were set and a secretary was employed. In the preamble to their revised charter, six objectives were set forth:

1. Shortening of the time necessary to eject an undesirable tenant

2. Compiling a record of undesirable tenants

3. Eliminating the "obnoxious" features of the OPA rental program

4. Beginning of test cases against the OPA if necessary

5. Joining a national landlord organization

6. Working for the benefit of a good tenant's interests as well as those of the landlord[93]

In response to the landlords, Crill agreed that rents in the city on the control date, March 1, 1942, were low but the action taken was designed to prevent inflation and that the law of supply and demand no longer operated in Sioux Falls. He argued that the general net income of landlords was higher under rent control than before because of the absence of vacancies. There would not be a general increase in rental fees until it could be shown that increased costs had more than eliminated the increases in net income.[94]

Although the rental fee problem was solved, most landlords, during the duration of World War II, were reluctant to rent houses to soldiers because they were subject to transfer. One soldier, looking for a place to live, provided a life history and character references, promised to pay his rent in advance and agreed to buy furniture. The landlady asked if he had any children. He replied, "I have one child." When hearing this, the landlady hung up the receiver with a deafening crack before he could say that the child was only five weeks old and not likely to cause any damage. Another house the soldier sought was said to have been rented to a man who paid six months' rent in advance. He had no luck with another landlord who picked his tenants from a list of twenty five.[95]

The housing problem continued throughout the remainder of World War II. Six hundred couples applied at the Base Housing Office in June, July and August of 1945, but only 204 found apartments. Some of the apartments provided few of the comforts associated with a normal home. One ad in the *Argus Leader* listed an unfurnished garage house, heating, stove, water and garbage service furnished, renting for $17.33 a month. Many landlords wanted to rent only to civilians after hearing rumors that the base would soon close and military personnel would be redeployed, reassigned or discharged from the service. Many military men who were transferred left their families in Sioux Falls. They did not want to spend months looking for a place to live again.[96]

Other GI gripes included the misrepresenting of services by landlords. Some rental ads included available natural gas for heating and cooking but neglected to inform military families that they had to drop a quarter in the meter every time they wanted to use gas. There were landlords who objected to daily bathing and set a limit for tenants of one bath a week. One landlord told a soldier that his wife could only take three baths a week and he could wash at the ATS.

There were landlords who preferred civilian renters for other reasons. The problem was that a small minority of soldiers' wives were considered very poor housekeepers. Landlords complained of military wives ignoring requests to dispose of garbage. A wife had indicated she would provide bed linens but she slept under the mattress cover and ruined the mattress. Soldiers' wives smoked in bed and burned holes in mattresses. They damaged furniture and woodwork. Active children also caused problems. They roller skated in the house and ruined floors. A five-year-old child pulled up the landlady's aster plants. There were abundant petty gripes and complaints by both military personnel and landlords. In fairness to Sioux Falls landlords, it must be said that many officers and men were amazed at the low rents in Sioux Falls compared to other parts of the country. When renting rooms for $25 per month, they indicated that it cost twice as much in other parts of the country. GIs complained about the petty details, believing that all soldiers were being judged by the actions of a few. At the same time, the great majority of the city's landlords, who tended to be hospitable and congenial, were being judged by the actions of a few who, through personal rules and regulations, alienated GI renters.[97]

Like most American cities that hosted newly constructed military bases, Sioux Falls muddled through the war meeting, wherever possible, the housing needs of the thousands of servicemen and civilian personnel who descended upon the city seeking suitable living quarters for their spouses and families. Although there were occasional crises, the citizens of Sioux Falls handled in a workmanlike and positive way the new challenges created by having thousands of military personnel in their midst. Granted, the servicemen had their usual gripes and the citizens their usual complaints but, overall, the relations between town and air base were very good. Sioux Falls proved to be one of the best towns a GI ever experienced.

# Chapter 3

## COMMAND

*Duty, Honor, Country – Motto of the U.S.*
*Military Academy at West Point*

General policy for any military base in the United States was determined by superiors in the War Department and the Secretary of the Army, Henry L. Stimson. Prior to the entry of the United States into the war, many career officers were unable to break through the promotion ceiling because the peacetime army was small, the country had experienced the Great Depression, and many excellent officers had to wait for those above them to retire. In 1939, the American Army ranked 19th among the world's armed forces—behind Portugal but ahead of Bulgaria. The active Army numbered 174,000 men with only three organized divisions. Congress had continually reduced appropriations for the Army and the Chief of Staff, General George C. Marshall, said that Congress "had reduced the Army to the status of that of a third rate power" with less than 25 percent readiness to fight.[1] By 1941, with war raging in East Asia and Europe, Marshall tempered his criticism of Congress because the Army acknowledged itself subordinate to the civil power. Beginning with the motto first learned at the U.S. Military Academy at West Point, "Duty, Honor, Country," the operating concept of the officer corps was duty. A bylaw of the West Point Association of Graduates was "There shall be no discussion of politics."[2] In September 1940, Congress enacted the first peacetime draft in American history and the build-up of armed forces began to create new opportunities to advance in rank for men such as Colonel Roy W. Camblin and his successor, Colonel Narcisse L. Cote.

## COLONEL NARCISSE L. COTE

Assigned to bring order to what appeared to be a chaotic situation at the Army Technical School in Sioux Falls was Colonel Cote. He assumed command of the Sioux Falls base on July 10, 1942, five days after classes had begun. Within a year, he was to build the Sioux Falls Army Air Forces Technical School into the Number One radio school in the United States. A career military man, he enlisted in the Army Air Forces in 1923. Of French Canadian descent, he was familiar with the perplexing problems faced by soldiers because he had come up through the ranks. Cote was commissioned a Second Lieutenant in 1926 at Maxwell Field, Alabama. After six years at this post, he was transferred to Brooks Field, San Antonio, Texas, where he commanded an aviation squadron. This was followed by three and one-half years of service at Nichols Field, near Manila, in the Philippine Islands.

Colonel Narcisse L. Cote, Commanding Officer, July 10, 1942-July 9, 1943. *Center for Western Studies.*

His last assignment before being transferred to Sioux Falls was at Scott Field, Illinois, where he was Director of Training. According to *Argus Leader* reporter Ted Ramsey, Colonel Cote was not pleased at being sent to Sioux Falls. He wanted to command a flying unit. Ramsey indicated that Cote "thought Sioux Falls was the North Pole of the universe." It was Cote who selected the name "Polar Tech" for the base newspaper.[3] Nevertheless, the Air Force veteran, who called for a formal inspection of the base on the morning of his arrival, was diplomatic in his remarks to the citizens of Sioux Falls. He commented, "From what I have learned, everyone in the service has been pleasantly accommodated here in Sioux Falls and they have been assisted in every way."[4]

The men and women under his command would develop mixed views concerning his leadership qualities. In late October 1942, he was seen dressed in coveralls and fatigues assisting fellow officers unload eight boxcar loads of canned goods into the base warehouse as part of the officers' physical conditioning program. Officers had to go through the program as did an enlisted man. The Colonel, it was said, acted as overseer and moved two boxes to every man's one.[5]

His policy concerning absent without leave (AWOL) soldiers was indicative of his stern and disciplined leadership. In the January 29, 1943, edition of *Polar Tech*, he reminded the men under his command of the consequences of going AWOL. Under the headline "A Word of Caution," he wrote, "Many men now in confinement are there because they felt their particular case would not receive the understanding it deserved. Furloughs are based on emergencies and the need for recuperation after long hours and meritorious performance of duty. They are not issued on mere request of a soldier. Students are given furlough in case of emergency only. Every soldier owes it to himself and to his country to forget his personal desires and remember that we have a war still to be won."[6]

Paul Graves, a non-commissioned officer, who had been at the base prior to its opening, thought Colonel Cote to be an eccentric character. He observed that the Colonel liked to run the little gasoline switch engine that moved boxcars on the side track in the warehouse area. Cote would ride up and down the track blowing the engine's whistle. Graves commented that "Cote thought that it was a big deal."[7]

Cote was notorious for changing the dress code from day-to-day. Soldiers would have to walk a half-mile to Gate Two to secure transportation into the city. They would find out at the gate that the dress code for the day had been changed. They would walk back to their barrack to change their uniforms. By that time it was too late to go into the city. Usually, the Class A code was required off of the base. Wearing an overseas cap was not permitted. They were prohibited from wearing their helmets, but the helmet liner was required.

Following a brief rain shower, Colonel Cote ordered men leaving the base to wear galoshes despite the likelihood that fifteen minutes after the shower there might be dust blowing. The soldiers had a knack for ditching the galoshes in certain places as they went downtown. Knowing of Cote's proclivities to change the uniform of the day, military policemen (MPs) usually looked the other way as base personnel walked down Phillips Avenue sans galoshes.[8]

The first issue of *Polar Tech*, which was printed by the *Argus Leader*, contained an article not to the Colonel's liking. He wanted to kill the issue. It had already been sent to off-base subscribers, but he refused to have the paper delivered at the base. After the editor of the *Argus Leader* made revisions in the story, the paper was delivered to the base.[9]

Colonel Cote was a charming man when he gathered with some of the city's leading citizens at banquets, formal dances and when he played host to reporters and columnists visiting the base. On one occasion, when a group of visiting newspaper men had finished their dinner at one of the base's mess halls, the visitors lit up cigarettes. They ignored signs on the walls that forbade smoking in the building. An editor sitting near the Colonel asked if he might smoke. Cote's immediate response was, "No." The editor replied, "Look around you." As Cote did, he said, "Well, we will have to make an exception tonight." And then he also smoked.[10]

Cote, as a public relations gesture, asked twelve men from the Sioux Falls Senior Chamber of Commerce to fly over the base and surrounding area in small, two-seat planes. The members were impressed with the camouflage used to hide certain military installations and equipment. After their ride, the members were fed the rations that the enlisted men received.[11]

During a Mardi Gras celebration, Colonel Cote, along with hundreds of merry makers in costume or formal dress packed the main floor of the Sioux Falls Coliseum. Scores of soldiers were also present. One partying soldier made a social error. He intruded when Cote was saying goodnight to Governor M. Q. Sharpe, who was about to leave the Coliseum. The soldier, celebrating his scheduled departure for Officer's Training School, addressed the commanding officer hilariously and unnecessarily. The Colonel, with a forced smile, coolly shook the GI reveler's hand and firmly said, "Where's your blouse?" He added, "You have a great opportunity before you. I hope you do nothing to spoil it."[12]

Colonel Cote may have had some personality quirks but he had been assigned to the Sioux Falls ATS to do a job and he did it remarkably well. In one year, an Army Air Forces installation, still under construction when Cote arrived, was to be recognized as a first-rate Army Technical School.[13] Positive changes in curriculum occurred, new training techniques were introduced, new equipment arrived and classes were held twenty-four hours per day, seven days a week.

The views concerning Cote's leadership qualities among men and women under his command were mixed. In early July 1943, Colonel Cote became the commanding officer at Boca Raton, Florida. On July 9, 1943, after hearing of Cote's new assignment in the Army Air Forces Technical Training Command, the editor of *Polar Tech* had nothing but praise for Cote's administration. Cote, he wrote, "was a stern and hard driving CO. He built the Sioux Falls ATS into the Number One radio school. He worked unreasonable hours, more than he expected his men to work. Nothing less than perfection satisfied him. His results speak for themselves. Enlisted men always came first. He learned the details of every job on an Army post and there isn't a single assignment he cannot perform himself. Our dynamic commander was a great CO. We're going to miss him."[14]

## COLONEL OSCAR L. ROGERS

Colonel F. H. Robinson, who had enlisted in the Air Force in 1925, was acting base commander for one month after Cote's departure. He had been Director of Training for six months. Colonel Oscar L. Rogers was appointed as commanding officer on August 4, 1943, but did not assume command until September 9, 1943. With the arrival of his successor, Robinson was ordered to Maxwell Field, Alabama, for an undisclosed assignment. Colonel Rogers was to be base commander for seventeen months, from September 9, 1943, to March 1, 1945.

He had been the former commanding officer at Truex Field, Madison, Wisconsin. Forty-nine years old, Rogers had served twenty-seven years in the Air Force. He had been in charge of the Radio-Mechanics School at Madison. A native of North Carolina and a graduate of Weaver College, a Methodist institution, he had taught school for several years before enlisting in the Army Air Corps just

Colonel Oscar L. Rogers, Commanding Officer, September 9, 1943-March 1, 1945. *Center for Western Studies.*

prior to the entry of the United States into World War I.[15] South Dakota rabbit became one of his favorite dishes. He commented that "the cottontails here have a sweeter flavor and are much more tender than those we have down south."[16]

In most matters, he carried out base operations as established by Colonel Cote. His principal interest was reorganization of the base units. Two months after his arrival, he reorganized the curriculum. He created three divisions of responsibility: (1) He formed an Operational Training Division, charged with all phases of advanced training of the students up to the time they left the base. (2) He created a new Specialized Training Branch, a Radio Mechanics Division, for students graduating solely as Radio Mechanics. (3) He established a Service Division to expedite work formerly done by the Instructional Aids Branch, Supply Division and the Drafting and Reproduction Division.[17]

On April 30, 1944, Rogers ordered a massive reorganization of the Army Air Forces' base units with their numerical designations. He would have four main assistants to carry out command functions. There were to be Deputies for Administration and Service, Training and Operations and Supply and Maintenance. The other deputy was the Air Inspector. The new organization was intended to reduce paperwork.

The Signal Corps and Ordnance and Chemical Warfare units were placed directly under Supply and Maintenance. There would be no more Technical School Squadrons. As of May 1, they were designated as Sections with various letters for identification. The Headquarters Section would make up a large part of Section A. Instructors in the Radio School and flying personnel formed Section B. Section C consisted of Supply and Maintenance personnel. The WACS were assigned to Section D. Section E was the Medical Detachment and Section F was the 85th Aviation Squadron and the 929 Quartermaster Platoon (under the command of Captain J.E. Shannon).[18] The Inspector General's Department gave the Sioux Falls Army Technical School an excellent rating in its quarterly inspection. Colonel Rogers said that in his quarter of a century in the Army he

Staff meeting at a local hotel. Colonel Oscar Rogers is dressed in the light-colored uniform and smoking a pipe. *Courtesy Dave Kemp.*

had never found a group of men superior to those stationed at the Sioux Falls Army Technical School.

## Other Commanders

On March 1, 1945, when Colonel Rogers traveled to Washington D.C., for a special fourteen-week course for staff officers, command of the Army Technical School fell to a series of officers. The first of Rogers' successors was Colonel Raymond J. Reeves. A West Point graduate, he arrived on the base during the last week in February 1945. He served as Deputy Commander and was Rogers' replacement as commander for three weeks.[19] Reeves was relieved of his command by Colonel Louie C. Mallory in late March 1945. He arrived in Sioux Falls from the Columbus, Mississippi, Army Air Field where he had been commanding officer since 1941.[20]

A significant change took place at the base on June 1, 1945, when it came under the command of the 2nd Air Force. On June 1, 1945, Colonel Sig R. Young became the first officer to direct the transition of the Sioux Falls base from a Radio School to a deployment center. The war had ended in Europe on May 8 and many men from that theater of operations were being deployed to East Asia with preparations being made for the invasion of the Japanese home islands. Young was a veteran B-17 pilot with twelve months of action against the Nazis. He, like so many of his predecessors, had come up through the ranks, enlisting as a private in 1936. He entered cadet flying training in October 1937 and was commissioned a Second Lieutenant in 1938.

During his brief time as commander, Young ordered an emphasis on military courtesy, particularly off-base. A Base Security Detail, under the Provost Marshal, aided the military police during patrol duty on Saturday nights. Most discrepancies were in uniform

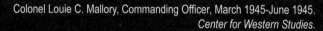

Colonel Louie C. Mallory, Commanding Officer, March 1945-June 1945.
*Center for Western Studies.*

Colonel Sig R. Young, Commanding Officer, June 1, 1945-June 30, 1945.
*Center for Western Studies.*

violations—sleeves rolled up, some men without head covering while others were wearing service caps not authorized by the Base, ties not tight to the collar and a few men needing haircuts.[21] Young was replaced by Colonel John R. Kane in early July. A holder of the Congressional Medal of Honor, Kane took part in the first bombing of the Ploesti oil fields in Rumania.[22] Kane had been at the Sioux Falls base for only a few weeks when Brigadier General Shepler W. Fitzgerald was designated the commanding officer on July 21, 1945. Fitzgerald had been commander of the African Middle East Wing of the Air Transport Command and the U.S. Army Air Forces in Central Africa. He was rated as a command pilot and combat observer. There is no evidence, however, that Fitzgerald ever served at the Sioux Falls base.[23]

The actual successor to Colonel Kane was Brigadier General Robert F. Travis. By this time, the war in the Pacific had ended with

Colonel John R. Kane, Commanding Officer, June 1, 1945-July 21, 1945.
*Center for Western Studies.*

the Japanese surrender on August 14, 1945. It was General Travis who announced that the Sioux Falls base would be deactivated on December 31, 1945.[24] After Travis was transferred to Sioux City, Iowa, he was replaced by Colonel George A. Blakey in November 1945. Colonel Philippe Foote arrived and departed in a scant two weeks prior to deactivation. Official deactivation took place on the last day of December 1945. A second lieutenant was assigned to handle the disposition of property.

Why were eight different officers assigned to the Sioux Falls base as commanders during its last eight months of active status? The change in the base's functions accounts for some of the changes. Certainly, the overlying cause was the culmination of World War II with the surrender of Japan. There was no need for the further deployment of men to the East Asian theater of operations. Second, with the end of World War II, the once training school and deployment center became a separation center. Thousands of men were discharged from the military service at the base. Third, the officers who briefly served as base commanders were undergoing a transition in their careers. There was the option of retirement but the majority of these men looked forward to reassignment to a stateside or overseas base. Sioux Falls was a temporary holding area until they or their superiors in Washington, D.C., determined their future.

# Chapter 4

*Students in the radio school tell us Paul Revere was America's first radio man. He broadcast on one plug.*
*– Polar Tech, November 12, 1943*

Preparations for receiving the first group of trainees proceeded at astonishing speed with several days of dry weather in early June. Construction had been hampered by a very wet spring and the site of the new Army Technical School (ATS) was a sea of mud. Colonel Camblin declared that the rate of arrival of students depended upon the completion of facilities. By mid-June 1942, barracks to house 5,000 men were completed and ready for occupancy. Conditions were still quite primitive as road maintainers were being used to create new streets. The first detachment of officers and non-commissioned officers had already arrived in Sioux Falls to organize and activate the base. Until there was housing available at the Army's newest technical school, they used the Sioux Falls Coliseum and its annex for their offices, dining and sleeping quarters.

As construction continued in Sioux Falls, future instructors for the base were involved in a ten-day training program at the Instructor Training Division (ITD) at Scott Field, Illinois. Since December 1941, the Training Command had established branches in Chicago, Grand Rapids, Michigan, Sparta and Madison, Wisconsin, and now at Sioux Falls, South Dakota. The ITD was the source of all instruction in radio operating and radio mechanics. Enlisted men and civilians sat side-by-side learning and working together. After completing the course, the future instructors were able to teach all phases of radio mechanics, including courses in radio fundamentals and aircraft radio equipment. From Scott Field, the new instructors proceeded to Sioux Falls to establish a school for local instructors with two primary objectives in mind. First, to train potential instructors from a technical point of view and, second, to provide personnel qualified as instructors with in-service training on a continuing basis.[1]

Local citizens who were accepted as potential instructors underwent a condensed but rigorous thirty-day training program. Coursework included a mechanics course that covered all phases of radio mechanics techniques, instructions in teaching methods, speech and visual education and a primary emphasis on practice teaching. The soon-to-be instructors were required to present subject matter in every aspect of radio training.

Of major importance was coursework in code, tactical procedures and blinkers. As soon as they could take sixteen words per minute in code, they were assigned to a class, which consisted of 425 to 450 men. Code work consisted of code receiving and sending, short exercises and blinker drills. A goal was to have small classes, since limiting the number of students per class enabled trainees to finish the course in a minimal amount of time.[2]

The first students began class work on July 6, 1942, while sawdust and wood chips were still in the air. In basic training, the men had been tested for their technical aptitude to see if they qualified for radio school. They marched over muddy streets to classes in the barracks and ate in partly equipped mess halls. The large classroom buildings were still under construction while contractors were finishing dozens of barracks per day. Many of the men who arrived first at the new ATS had "washed out" of pilot training. Most of the first contingent had a college or university education. Some of the men were lawyers, medical doctors or college professors. They wanted to fly and if they had failed as navigators their next stop was

Back entrances to the classroom buildings in the center of the Army Air Base. *Center for Western Studies.*

radio school. If they failed to graduate from radio school, they were assigned to gunnery schools in Yuma, Arizona, Panama City, Florida, or Las Vegas, Nevada. Ultimately, they were assigned to one of the "bubble stations" on a B-17 or a B-24, the most perilous positions in aerial combat as they were susceptible to ground-based anti-aircraft batteries.[3] Nevertheless, no matter what their status, these men wanted to be part of an air crew. Assigned to bring order to what appeared to be a chaotic situation was Colonel Narcisse L. Cote. Colonel Cote assumed command of the base on July 10, 1942, five days after classes had begun. As stated earlier, within a year, he was to build the Sioux Falls Army Technical School into the Number One radio school in the United States.

The ATS took recruits from an above-average group determined under the Army's General Classification Test. Most of the men assigned to the Radio School scored 100 or higher on the Classification Test. The initial goal was to produce qualified radio men after an eighteen-week basic course. The Army pointed out that the cost of such radio training for a civilian in a regular school would be more than $1,000.[4] The daily schedule for the trainees, with some minor adjustments, remained the same from July 1942 to September 1945.

## Army Technical School Daily Schedule

| First Shift | Military Time | Civilian Time |
|---|---|---|
| First Call | 0500 | (5:00 AM) |
| Reveille | 0510 | (5:10 AM) |
| Mess Formation | 0500-0645 | (5:00-6:45 AM) |
| School | 0700-1015 | (7:00-10:15 AM) |
| Mess Formation | 1015-1115 | (10:15-11:15 AM) |
| School | 1115-1430 | (11:15AM-2:30 PM) |
| Physical Training | 1500-1620 | (3:00 PM-4:20 PM) |
| Squadron Duty | 1620-1720 | (4:20-5:20 PM) |
| Mess Formation | 1720-1830 | (5:20-6:30 PM) |
| Individual Recreation | 1830-2030 | (6:30-8:30 PM) |
| Taps | 2045 | (8:45 PM) |
| Bed Check | 2115 | (9:15 PM) |

Maintenance people came in and cleaned up the classroom before the arrival of the next shift.[5]

In mid-September 1942, a "graveyard" or night shift was established. Now operating on three shifts, in the latter part of October the school went on a seven-day work week, twenty-four hours per day. With this schedule, 10 to 15 percent would be granted a day off during the week instead of an entire class being free on Sunday. There would be no overflow of soldiers downtown during weekends. The same number of men would not be free each day because of the varying size of the squadrons at the ATS.[6]

## THE ELECTRICAL FUNDAMENTALS DIVISION

**Dirge of the Radio Man**
*I think that I shall never know*
*A thing about the radio.*
*Oh radio, your parts will be*
*Forever just a mystery.*
*I gazed at you in silent awe,*
*My mouth-ajar-for what I saw*
*Will haunt me to the day I die.*
*Oh radio, I ask you—why?*
*To me you will no longer be*
*A source of pleasant company,*
*Oh radio, you irk me so,*
*I guess you know where you can go.*
*– Private Edward H. Blueter*

The curriculum for aspiring radio operator-mechanics (ROMs) consisted of two courses of study: Electrical and Radio Fundamentals. The steam-heated classrooms were ready to be occupied by the students on September 13, 1942. Classes up until that time had been held in the barracks. A new student, on his first day at the base, was presented with a fighter pilot's radio set, lab benches and "breadboards." With all of the foregoing in front of him, he had a good look at a compact aircraft command set. Louis Warren, a local instructor and later an academic inspector, designed the flexible circuit board. Warren commented that the average education of his first class recruits was 4.5 years of college, and contained several medical doctors, lawyers and other professional men.

Students learning (or attempting to learn) to assemble their radios on the "breadboards." *Center for Western Studies.*

The first radio mechanics' classes were conducted through lectures. Initially, lacking adequate equipment, the course was theoretical and trainees learned about radios on paper. They drew circuit diagrams and solved problems for homework. The only radio parts available for demonstration were donated by local citizens in salvage drives. By August 1, 1942, tubes, condensers and coils began to appear in the classroom.

Headphones, transmitting machines and switchboards arrived in September. Following an inspection by Major General Walter A. Weaver, the commander of the Army Air Forces Training Command, the mechanics courses were to stress "hands on learning." Overnight, the mechanics classes were changed from theory courses to classes in which demonstration or student participation was emphasized. Students now learned about electricity and radio from their own breadboard equipment and did their wiring on equipment instead of drawing diagrams on paper. Class Number 20 was the first to enter the new mechanics course as the school went to a seven-day, round-the-clock training week.

Students were assigned to one of three groups of school squadrons. GIs in each barrack would follow the same daily schedule. Everybody in the same barrack was in the same shift but not necessarily in the same class. There were people coming and going at all hours, day and night, all over the base. The mess halls were open twenty-four hours a day. For men going off-base, the curfew was set for midnight except for Saturday when all soldiers must have returned to the base by 2:00 A.M. Sunday morning.[7]

Students began at the bottom of the electrical ladder and worked their way to the top. Their knowledge of alternating current, vacuum tubes and the other phases of the electrical process were reorganized with a greater emphasis on testing and repair of equipment. The students studied five phases of radio theory. They were introduced to molecular electronics and Ohm's Law, the main underpinnings of the radio. They engaged in intensive study of direct current, alternating current, vacuum tubes, transmitters and receivers.[8] Ohm's Law states that the resistance of a circuit determines the amount of current that will flow under a given difference of potential. The electric current, the difference of potential and resistance can all be expressed through the following familiar units: current in amperes, resistance in ohms, and difference of potential in volts. At every point in the course, the actual operation and demonstration of equipment was stressed in preference to lectures. If a soldier was told that a vacuum tube amplifies, he plugged in one of the tubes and listened to the amplified sound. If told that a transformer steps current up or down, he checked the result with a bench meter.[9]

Overall, students mastered the five phases of theory through practical application. The Aircraft Radio Division (ARD) lab had every piece of communication equipment found on military aircraft. They learned to read wiring diagrams in reverse, to examine a set and to draw a diagram of its electrical design. The air-minded GIs became familiar with the Air Force's standard system of filing technical information, the tech order system. They were also taught the use of the radio compass and the command set which pilots used for aircraft-to-aircraft and aircraft-to-ground communication.[10] Students in the Radio Mechanics course were required to maintain a grade average of 90 percent.[11]

Instructor's had different areas of responsibility. One might teach Radio Theory, where another instructor taught the students the theory of a superheterodyne receiver and assigned each one to build a working model. Students also learned the theory of an MOPA transmitter and built one. During the fifth week of instruction, students worked on the BC-348 receiver and the 275 or 375 transmitter used on B-17 bombers. The #375 transmitter was about 18" wide,

24" high and 6" or 8" deep. It had several 6" high vacuum tubes in it, a very large set compared to the hand-held instruments one can transmit on today.[12]

Location of his aircraft was an important part of the student's final test. The GIs took the test as though they were alone in a bomber radio compartment with disaster holding the stopwatch. A student had to tune in three stations on the radio compass set and find his position on the map within a few minutes. By May 1943, the men were also using a special radio compass to aid in navigation. Finding the location of a plane was called "shooting a bearing."[13] In mid-July 1943, new courses were added to the curriculum, Navigation Equipment I and II. In Navigation I, students learned specific aids to help guide a plane to and from a target. Included was information on the British "Standard Beam Approach": a system of blind landing whereby a pilot could land his plane in bad weather. Navigation II was a revision of the radio compass course.[14]

The course of study proved difficult for many of the trainees. Adhering to a directive from Training Command one hour was added to the daily schedule to be used for supervised study. The study hour was not to be interrupted by duty assignments not pertaining to technical training. There were to be no disturbances or distractions.[15] These official "get together" sessions were for students held back in both the Electronic Fundamental and Radio Fundamental branches of study. Students who failed final exams had to attend these sessions. They met with a school officer and one or more examiners to discuss individual cases. It was emphasized that the sessions were not in any way punitive but designed to help the students in areas in which they were weak.[16]

Obviously, there were students with time on their hands: Lewis W. Powsner and Morton Wiener, the Funk and Wagnalls of the Sioux Falls Army Technical School, published a new Radio Dictionary which included the following definitions:

Ampere – Where civilians threw their soiled clothes

Volt – Where the folks back home store their war bonds

Ohm – Be it ever so 'umble, there's no place like it

Ion – What the GI laundry doesn't use on our shirts

Frequency – What? Beans again?

Inductive Reactance – How did you feel when the doctor said you passed?

Mutual Inductance – When a fellow gets his draft papers the day before he was going to enlist anyway

Duo-diode – For dear old Rutgers

## RADIO FUNDAMENTALS DIVISION

*It used to be the bugle call*
*That got us out of bed*
*But something has been added to*
*Go buzzing through our head*

*It's not that we can sleep at night*
*When we first hit the hay*
*But during code we spent our time*
*In sleeping half the day.*

*We wake up in the morning*
*The dawn's first beam of light*
*But now we're on thirty words*
*We stay up half the night.*

*But code alone doesn't make us gripe*
*For theory does its part*
*We all know what a cathode is*
*Where electrons get their start.*

*– Polar Tech*, November 12, 1943

Students were trained to communicate via the international Morse code.  In 1844, inventor Samuel F.B. Morse sent the first message in his code over a telegraph wire from Washington D.C. to Baltimore, a distance of thirty miles.  The message was "What hath God wrought?"  In 1943, the Morse code was the only means of communication over a long distance.

The radio operator at this time used an old-fashioned telegraph key mounted on a small desk in the airplane. The key was like a light switch. It closed a circuit in the radio transmitter which sent out a solid tone radio signal. The Morse code established a uniform system of letter and digit identification using dots and dashes. "A" was "dot-dash." "B" was "dash, dot, dot, dot." "C" was "dash, dot, dash, dot." Depressing the telegraph key for a short period of time produced a dot; depressing the key for a longer period of time produced a dash. The students called them "dit-dahs."

The radio operator's job was to keep in touch with the ground command.[17] He provided information as to the plane's current position and weather reports and operated the identification radar. An antenna hung from the plane while in flight. During over-water flights, the navigator used an octant or sextant to "shoot" the stars or sun to determine the plane's location. The Air Force stopped using the Morse code around 1957. The Code was officially abandoned in 2000.[18]

Until mid-September 1942, trainees learned to receive code sent by hand over a loudspeaker as equipment was scarce. Prior to September 13, there were only two shifts per day, morning and

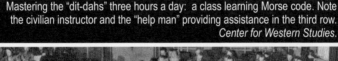
Mastering the "dit-dahs" three hours a day: a class learning Morse code. Note the civilian instructor and the "help man" providing assistance in the third row.
*Center for Western Studies.*

REVEILLE FOR SIOUX FALLS

Acquiring knowledge of long-distance radio equipment at the ATS.
*Center for Western Studies.*

afternoon, each equally divided between learning code and radio mechanics. By the end of September, the necessary equipment had arrived. Using the large classroom buildings, seventy men, divided into two classes, received instruction at the same time. Eventually, classes were composed of twenty to twenty-five students. There were three shifts: one from 7:00 A.M. to 2:30 P.M., another from 3:00 P.M. to 10:30 P.M. and a night shift beginning at 11:00 P.M. and concluding at 6:45 A.M. The first two shifts swapped shifts every other month whereas the night shift remained constant.

The code machines put out nearly three million dits and dahs in the course of a normal training day. Through his headset, the average student heard only about 31,000 of them in his classroom. The dits and dahs were arranged to make up codes varying from four to seventy words per minute. The letters of the alphabet were represented by dots and dashes. A student was provided with the code speed best suited to his ability within sixty seconds.[19] Students talked about their Groups Per Minute (GPM). Words were five-character groups of random letters and numbers which simulated the way students would be receiving and sending messages in operating situations since everything was encoded.[20] The goal was to master eighteen to twenty groups per minute.

After the first twelve days of class, students were expected to have learned four words per minute. By the twentieth day, they were expected to be up to eight words per minute. After less than eighty-five hours of instruction, the trainees were required to take ten words per minute.[21]

The ROM course began as an eighteen-week course but as noted earlier, in September 1943, it became a twenty-week course and it was eventually lengthened to twenty-six weeks. Eighteen words per minute became the requirement for graduation.[22] The need for new air crews to replace crews shot down in aerial combat over Europe led to lower requirements for graduation. In February 1944, the code requirement was reduced to fourteen words per minute. It was soon recognized that the fourteen-word requirement was inadequate, and at the end of July 1944 the course was lengthened to twenty-six weeks. Statistical studies indicated that the average student, with the "washbacks" counted in, required twenty-six weeks to attain the required proficiency for graduation. The requirement of an eighteen-word a minute in code had been the chief reason for student "washbacks."[23]

The first effort to train students for flight conditions while on the ground involved restructuring the mid-section of the fuselage of a B-17 bomber. This indoor mock-up marked the site of the radio compartment. It contained a transmitter and receiver. When in operation, advanced students would experience black-out, sub-zero and rough weather conditions. Night flight was simulated by blacking out the compartment except for dial lamps. Rough weather was simulated by rocking and rolling the fuselage section in its movable cradle. Cold weather operations were created by opening windows in the room and the top of the bomber section. Two students would be in the compartment at one time. They communicated with people outside of the compartment solely with their transmitters and receivers. Aircraft operational procedures were observed. Although primitive when compared to twenty-first-century technology, twenty of these simulators were to be constructed.[24]

The learning environment for students was gradually improved. Students no longer had to stand while operating their set. Permanent

The front sections of salvaged B-17s and B-24s being used as training stations while mastering the code. The radio man had his station in back of the pilot and co-pilot. *Center for Western Studies.*

benches were provided for each booth, and partitions were erected between the booths. Thus, students could now pay attention to their own work and were less likely to observe how their neighbors were getting along. When sufficient instructors became available, it was possible for each student to work with an individual instructor. A sliding panel was placed between the trainee and his instructor and communication between the two was almost entirely by radio. Exams, which lasted forty-five minutes, consisted of transmitting at 12, 14 and 16 words per minute and receiving at 12, 14 and 18 words per minute. There were written exams covering practical operating procedures and a radio mechanics check on equipment.[25]

By October 1944, the hulks of former B-17s and B-24s were being used to train students. The ATS had obtained the hulks of four B-17s, two B-24s and one B-25. All trainees became familiar with these mock fuselages before they were assigned to a flight in a real plane.[26]

The landing field at ATS was revamped so that aircraft could be used to train students. Personnel were also trained to operate the air field properly via the control tower. This involved radio contact, visual flashing and a light communication blinker.[27]

Three Link Trainers were installed to aid pilots in improving their instrument flying, simple maneuvers, radio navigation and cross-country blind flying. It was a stationary machine filled with controls and instruments found in a plane. The Link Trainer could duplicate any aerial maneuvers up to 30 degrees and the instrumental maneuvers of a real plane.[28]

During the last week of July 1943, every radio student was told that he would get a taste of the "wild blue yonder." Fifty brand-new Cubs of the L2 type were now stationed at the base flying line and nineteen enlisted pilots had arrived to fly the L2s. Additional

Light aircraft assembled on the side of the runway after a recent snowfall.
*Courtesy Doug Uthe.*

Cub planes were ferried to Sioux Falls in the ensuing weeks. The first goal was that every student and his radio instructor would have at least one hour of radio work in the sky. Each Cub was equipped with a commercial transmitter and receiver which could be operated by voice or key from the back seat.[29-30] The radio set had a range of twenty-five miles. All flying was done in the vicinity of the Army Technical School. Students took their maiden flight within the last two weeks before graduation.[31]

Many of the men had never flown before and had to adjust to air travel. Private First Class Richard J. Suhay said he looked down for the first time when he was approximately 200 feet off the ground. He later remarked, "It was a funny feeling. I got to thinking there wasn't much holding me up. Then I went to work on the radio and, in a couple of minutes, I was having the time of my life."

The "classroom in the air" was soon transferred to larger aircraft: Lockheed Hudson bombers (AT-18s). The silver colored AT-18s flew a triangular course from Sioux Falls to Lafayette, Minnesota, and then flew 120 miles west to Bruce, South Dakota, and from Bruce returned to the air base in Sioux Falls. With the altimeter set at 8,000 feet, the converted bomber sped along at 180 miles per hour. The total flight time was one hour and fifty minutes. Each plane had seats for four students. Six flying hours were required before graduation.[32]

Larger aircraft, including B-17s and B-24s, were flown to the base to provide flight training for students who had demonstrated superior ability as radio operators. They were the recipients of advanced training. The flights were to help students overcome "mike fright," or "key fright," to adapt them to the motion of the plane and to familiarize them with operating radios in highly technical planes.[33] Four months later, in November 1943, flight missions were lengthened to three hours. The reason for the additional time in the air was to reduce fuel consumption, since take-offs and landings required a greater expenditure of fuel than cruising. New routes were established with Fargo, Des Moines, Minneapolis or Omaha being the turn-around point for each flight. During their twentieth week at ATS, trainees would go aloft twice, each time for a three-

Flight instruction in a Link Trainer. *Courtesy Doug Uthe.*

The "classrooms in the air" were the Lockhead Hudson bombers (AT-18s). The silver-colored planes were used until December 1944 when an air collision put an end to their use. *Courtesy Doug Uthe.*

hour mission. The flight to return from one of the turn-around cities noted above averaged between 530 and 580 miles.

In mid-August 1944, *Polar Tech* announced that the base had never had a plane accident during approximately 50,000 hours of flight training. Only three soldiers had met their deaths in auto and motorcycle accidents off-base.[34] This meritorious record was broken as two AT-18s collided in mid-air in December 1944 (see Chapter 6).[35]

In December 1944, the flight training program was changed once again. The flight line received twenty Douglas C-47s. After the necessary radio equipment was installed in the C-47s, they replaced the AT-18s still in service. Most of the C-47s had been flown for less than fifteen hours. Fifteen former combat pilots arrived in January 1945 for assignment to fly the C-47 classrooms. Each C-47 accommodated twelve to fifteen students and two instructors, double the number of men who had flown on the AT-18 flights. Well insulated, the C-47s were rather quiet and suitable for training radio students.[36]

The C-47s had a perfect flying record. They were flown from December 24, 1944, to May 10, 1945. Thirteen planes were used in daily operations, logging 4,104 flying hours and carrying more than 8,000 students. The average cruising speed was 175 miles per hour. Students were now flying four-hour missions, averaging 640 miles on each flight.[37]

## BLINKERS

Another important component of the trainees' education was the ability to send messages via blinker code. In November 1942, plans were made to construct four to six towers for this purpose.[38] At the top of the towers was an all-glass enclosure from which students would operate blinkers. Signaling was also possible from the catwalk around each tower.[39] Ultimately, there were eight blinker towers, looming 7,000 feet above the base. Colonel Cote flashed a typical official message, using the communication procedures of tactical bases and combat fields.[40] A primary purpose of the towers was to aid in direction finding for planes in flight. A radio man aboard a plane in flight could contact a central planning room at the base and request a position of bearing information that would guide him and the crew safely back to the base.[41]

To further facilitate blinker operations, the base had two radio-equipped trucks in which students in Net Operations would move from place to place acting as Net Control Stations for the blinker towers twenty-four hours a day. They were self-sufficient mobile radio units. They pulled their generators behind them in a trailer. Each unit had one transmitter and two receivers.[42]

A trainee examining his radio set before take-off. *Courtesy Doug Uthe.*

The direction-finding facilities used the model developed by the Army Air Forces in the European theater of operations. It was used for bomber pilots who were lost off the English coast. Blind landing equipment was installed for use in radio navigation classes in Building 300. Students learned how pilots used landing instruments.[43] In practice runs at the ATS, a liaison plane would call the central plotting room for information to guide them back to the base. The plotting room put three towers into operation. The towers then indicated where the plane's signal was coming from. In the plotting room, the information from the three towers was used to determine the exact location of the plane on a plotting map. This procedure was the opposite of the radio compass, which shot bearings on three known radio stations using the tower system. The procedure took place in one minute. The students had to know both methods for overseas duty.[44]

In August 1944, students were startled to hear German when attempting to receive a message. Base administrators had established a "Gestapo Unit" in the Net Operations Branch. Several "jamming"

REVEILLE FOR SIOUX FALLS

records had been transcribed in the Pacific and European theaters of operation. The purpose was to jam frequencies used by students in Net Operations to simulate the practice of enemy radio operators and train students to get their message through all obstacles, man-made and natural.[45]

There were often changes in requirements and the teaching staff. Between 1942 and 1945, changes were made in the weeks of instruction, increasing from eighteen to twenty-six. In late February 1944, requirements were lowered. The blinker requirement dropped from eight to five words per minute and the code sending requirement from sixteen to fourteen words per minute. The requirement of eighteen words per minute was seen as the chief reason for student "washbacks."[46] Two courses were dropped, Navigational Equipment and General Test Procedures. Later, the code-sending requirement was set once again at eighteen words per minute. Tapes were also made more realistic through the introduction of static and interference. Often the tapes were sped up, increasing the difficulty with which students could discern sound.

A large number of civilian instructors were replaced by sixty-six Women's Army Corps radio instructors. Five of the groups were assigned to various mechanic branches dealing with radio. The new WACs had been trained at the Midland Radio and Television School in Kansas City, Missouri. Their coursework consisted of six to seventeen weeks in radio theory and twenty weeks of code instruction. A Midland diploma required 325 hours of code and 109 hours of hand sending.[47]

Final revisions in code copying and sending occurred in March 1945. The new requirements included three minutes of errorless copying and sending at nineteen GPMs out of a five-minute check. There would be four characters per group rather than five. The requirement read, "An ability to receive at a speed of 228 consecutive characters without error in any three minutes of a five-minute test, such characters to be grouped in four character groups."[48] Another official memo, attempting to improve proficiency in errorless code receiving, stated an increase from one to two minutes of "solid" copying at eighteen GPM before granting students official credit for this speed.[49]

Private Frank Elliot was recognized as the fastest trainee to master the ATS curriculum. He could send code at a rate of forty words per minute and receive code at a speed of seventy words a minute. He was in one of the first classes to graduate from the Sioux Falls base and he was to remain at the base as an instructor.[50]

Private Arthur S. Johnson was stationed at the Army Technical School from December 5, 1942, to May 3, 1943. While engaged in his studies, he kept a daily journal that describes life at the base and his daily classroom experiences. The following brief excerpts from the journal relate his experiences with the radio operators-mechanics curriculum. He had contracted pneumonia shortly after his arrival and after a stay in the hospital he attended his class on December 15, 1942.

## From the Journal of Private Arthur S. Johnson, 1942-1943

December 15     Worked on series hookups on board with resistors on them. Went to code class afterward. Caught on pretty fast. Sort of fun.

December 21     Spent theory class on coils–fun. Passed my 4 words per minute. That was in 21 hours and give me about an 89. I also got an 89 in Direct Current (DC).

December 24     Up at 5:00 A.M. Had a test in AC/DC. Guess I did okay, got 92 percent.

December 27     Up at 6:30 A.M., chow and class. Started circuit components.

December 28     Darn it! Didn't pass WPM check.

December 31     Passed 8 WPM on 2nd try. Did it decisively.

January 3        Got a new teacher in circuit analysis, an all lecture course. Started 10 WPM.

January 14       Code a little better. I should be on 12 soon.

January 16       Started on receivers. Hooked up detector stage and heard KSOO. Some fun!

January 19       Almost passed 10 WPM, missed by one letter. (Passed it the next day.)

| | |
|---|---|
| February 2 | I passed 12 WPM yesterday after lunch. Today I started 14 WPM. Now they introduce static to make it more like actual operating conditions. I didn't care for the static. |
| February 3 | Took test in Theory. Hope I keep up my marks. Code fair. |
| February 10 | Last day of the first half of transmitter. Made a frequency chart. |
| February 13 | Talked about antennas and keying (sending code) today. Missed my 14 by 2 letters, but passed 12 WPM recheck and went to a gunnery talk after calisthenics. |
| February 16 | Passed 14 WPM. Had to fight for it. Hope I pass 16 tomorrow or the next day. |
| February 24 | We played around with frequency meters today. Code was no better. The darn tape was running faster than 20 WPM. |
| March 5 | Started on Liaison set N. 375. It is quite a big set. This was used for flying later. It was about 2 feet wide by 3 feet high and 6 or eight inches deep, and had big radio tubes in it. |
| March 6 | Had to wear our gas masks all day. During the first hour of code had them on our faces. It wasn't easy to see since I can't wear my glasses inside them because it makes them leak. They are a nuisance to carry around, but we might as well get used to it. Tuned up the 375 Xmitter, fun. |
| March 8 | Worked on Xmitter and receiver some more. The time really flies when we are in the lab. Still no good on 20 word checks. |
| March 16 | Went over for an aerial gunnery exam, but never saw a doctor since wearing glasses cuts you out. |

| | |
|---|---|
| March 20 | Passed 20 WPM on 3rd check, am trying to write 25 WPM. |
| March 26 | Started A/N 522 command set receiver. It was used for transmitting and receiving as well as code, and the large No. 375 was the long-distance code transmitter we used on long flights when we were out of voice range and crossing oceans. |
| April 17 | Spent some time on Aircraft Identification and copying code. Went to Tower No. 4 by the airport. Had some blinkers in the tower and passed 12 WPM. |
| April 25 | Easter Sunday. Went to Tower No. 5. Sent one message and received one and sat in the sun the rest of the session. Worked in Code Room the rest of the day. |
| April 27 | [Johnson's last day of school. He took tests, had his notebook reviewed and his code speeds rechecked. He then went to Tower No. 7 where he did some coding and recoding plus blinker practice.] Tomorrow we will be all through. It was nice to sign off for last time. |
| April 28 | Graduation day. Got up at 6:30 A.M. March down to the Coliseum. They seated us alphabetically. Then I was called up on the stage. I ranked 10th in the class. I got a special diploma. It indicated that I completed with Distinction the course for Radio Operator and Mechanics as presented by the Army Air Forces Technical Training Command. |

Private Johnson remained on the base until May 4 when he received orders to the 6th Ferrying Group of the Air Transport Command in Long Beach, California, as a flight radio operator. During the six days until his departure, he worked in the coal pile and in the Supply Room, moving overcoats. From Long Beach, Johnson was assigned to the SW Pacific Wing Air Transport Service flying C-47s out of Biak Island in New Guinea to Australia and the

Philippines. Lastly, he served on General MacArthur's Flight Section in Tokyo, Japan, from September 1945 until February 1946. Johnson was discharged on February 16, 1946.[51]

It was not true of every trainee, but Johnson was very satisfied with the ROM course he took at the Army Technical School. He said that the work was fascinating and that time really flew when engaged in his studies. He found the code also fascinating but thought that achieving twenty words per minute took forever. He commented that "A number of instructors were civilians and most were very nice." He had interesting lectures on radio theory and practice, and hands-on-work on circuit boards and actual sets: "It was fun building an elementary radio and getting reception."[52]

Students who had difficulty mastering the material had to participate in "help" sessions. They met with a school officer and one or more examiners to discuss individual cases. It was emphasized that the sessions were not in any way punitive but designed to help students in areas in which they were weak. Despite the "help" sessions, many students never completed the course. Some were reassigned to electronic school in Madison, Wisconsin, where they became radar mechanics. Others sought different assignments. Several students were sent to gunnery school. Several men could not take the cold and were often hospitalized at the base. The most unfortunate trainees were sent to Western Europe as replacements for American ground troops who suffered significant casualties following D-Day, June 6, 1944.

On April 27, 1945, with the total collapse of Nazi Germany, orders came from St. Louis that no new classes would begin at the Army Technical School until further notice. It meant the total suspension of entering classes. A surplus of radio operator-mechanics were piling up at gunnery schools because of the end of large-scale operations in Europe. Class No. 435 was the last class to enter the school. The class had begun training on April 16. The orders changed the mission of the base.[53] The Army Air Forces Training Command announced that the base would be taken over by the 2nd Air Force. The 2nd Air Force officially took over the base on June 1. On that date, all military personnel with the exception of radio instructors, students and aircraft maintenance men plus certain administrative personnel were transferred to the 2nd Air Force. All aircraft were to be removed and reassigned to the Eastern Technical Training Command.[54] The base was to become a redeployment center for transferring men from the European Sector of the war to the Pacific Sector or East Asia.

More than 45,000 radio operator-mechanics flowed through the base between July 6, 1942 and May 11, 1945: 161 classes entered and completed the course and graduated. In the European theater of World War II, it is estimated that more than 50 percent of ROM gunners were graduates of the school. By mid-summer 1944, the Sioux Falls Army Technical School was generally recognized as the Number One AAF radio school of its type in the United States.

# Chapter 5

## FIELD TRAINING AND FIELD WORK

*I'll travel a lot in the Army,*
*No matter where I roam*
*One thing I'll always try to do,*
*Is beat my dog-tags home.*
*- Polar Tech humor*

Colonel Cote, in the spring of 1943, ordered the establishment of a model advanced air base having an overseas atmosphere. The goal was to give students radio training under simulated field conditions. This specialized training would enhance the reputation of Sioux Falls radio operator-mechanics as being ready for duty upon assignment.[1] The Special Training Unit's quarters were located north of the landing field in a wooded area measuring 750' x 750'. In the center of the area was an operations office, message center and a communications office. The model air base was named after Staff Sergeant Howard L. Covert, a former instructor who was thought to have been the first Army Technical School casualty in the European theater of the war.[2] It was later discovered that he was a prisoner of war and housed in one of the Nazi stalags (prisoner-of-war camps).

## COVERT TRAINING UNIT

Three AT-12 planes and two B-25 Billy Mitchell bombers were dispersed under the trees. They had additional protection from a camouflage composed of burlap, paint and tree branches covering the area. At the four corners of the model base, four blinker towers were built and camouflaged as much as possible. Dummy anti-aircraft guns were placed at intervals and they were to be manned during alerts. All of the students taking training at the operational unit practiced air alert drills as though they were on guard overseas where an attack might take place at any moment. If an alarm sounded, two radio students would get into the cockpits of two of the planes and give the signal for take-off. Although the planes remained stationary, the students were to operate the radio sets in the planes as though they were on a flight in a combat zone.[3]

Student radio operators in the Covert Training Unit (CTU) improved their compass reading techniques in the two B-25 bombers. They received other training in Building 300 and the blinker control towers. Part of their training was spent at the local YMCA pool. In preparation for the possibility of being forced to abandon their plane over the English Channel or the North Sea, they were taught how to use barrack bags, shirts and trousers as water wings or floats for the injured. They were also taught proper methods for swimming through burning oil and debris.[4]

The Covert Training Unit was subjected to mock air attacks in July 1943. The attacking planes bombarded the area with sandbags and small bags of flour. There were also mock tear gas attacks, requiring the men on the ground to don gas masks while manning anti-aircraft guns and assigned battle stations. The tear gas and mock bombing raids became more frequent in early August. There were days when the unit's personnel were required to wear gas masks at all times.[5] Trainees practiced radio drills while seated in the three AT-12s as other trainees raced to slit trenches during the air raid drills.[6]

While alerts increased in number, the camouflage of the CTU was completed in August. From the air, the area looked like a large wood pile and a dumping ground for non-essential materials with additional burlap and chicken-wire screens. Leaves of artificial trees supplemented natural cover. Part of the regular road encircling the base was plowed under and another road constructed that circled hundreds of yards away from the unit's location. Coal was spread along the main road of the area to give the appearance of rutting truck tracks indicating from the air that they would not bear heavy traffic.[7]

In mid-August, 150 students were moved into the Covert area. Here they bivouacked, studied radio operating and maintenance under simulated combat conditions. Fifty members were trained in each of three daily shifts. The men lived in tents, ate from a field kitchen and otherwise functioned as if they were stationed at an overseas air base.[8]

During the last week in August 1943, the Covert Training Unit went on full-scale battle maneuvers. Only students who were in their last week of training were permitted to leave the unit for actual flight training. The students remaining in the CTU performed all of the tasks required for the operation of an isolated advance base such as guard and fatigue duty in addition to their radio work. The CTU was soon equipped to handle 450 men on a three shift basis. The schedule provided eight hours of fatigue and physical training, six hours of radio operating and maintenance and eight hours of sleep.

The planes at CTU never left the ground. Their operators, however, gave radio pre-flight inspections and called the CTU ground station for take-off instructions. While in simulated flight, radio operators received weather reports and sent the plane's position reports back to the ground station. Upon returning to base, the operator called for landing instructions.[9]

As was done in World War I, the Covert Training Unit received 150 Army pigeons. Students in their last week of training were shown how to care for pigeons aboard planes and how to release them in flight without injury. The trainees were also shown how to make out message forms and attach them to the pigeons' legs.[10]

The CTU at the Sioux Falls Army Technical School was abruptly discontinued in the first days of June 1944. The end came with a directive from Fort Worth, Texas, that all model overseas bases be disestablished at all technical schools. The directive stated that the enlisted technical student was to receive the equivalent of the field training in the basic training centers and at the Air Force Training Centers.[11]

## BASIC TRAINING

One year after classes began at the Army Technical School, a new directive from the Army Air Forces Technical Training Command required that all men must have at least one month of basic training before being shipped overseas. The training was similar to that given to new men in the armed services. On a typical day, there would be three hours of drill, one hour of physical training, two hours of lecture and forty-five minutes devoted to inspection in retreat. The climax of the course was a ten-mile overnight hike. No decision was made as to whether the manual of arms rifle drill would be included in the training.[12]

How closely the directive was followed is subject to question. When Major General Jacob Fickel, the Commanding General of the Army Air Forces Eastern Technical Training Command, visited the base, he expressed great unhappiness with the men's marching performance. The General said they needed to march like soldiers. The three hours of drill were to be enforced.[13]

The Physical Training (PT) involved exercise comparable to overseas training. It involved digging foxholes and trenches, rope climbing, running through an obstacle course that included climbing over a log wall and crawling under wire fencing. Students had to run the course at least once a month. Their efforts were timed by members of the Permanent Party. The course was located to the east of the present day Elmwood Golf Course.[14]

During the summer of 1943, Technical Training Command headquarters said that all enlisted personnel were to receive training in the use of pistols, rifles and sub-machine guns before being graduated from the radio school. In May 1943, the Army acquired 388.8 acres of the Lacy property east of Sioux Falls in the Cactus Heights area.[15] The site was used for small-caliber weapons training until it was declared surplus property on January 16, 1946. There was a twenty-target and sub-machine gun range and a special forty-target rifle range. Fifty percent of the men qualified as marksmen or better. The scores were listed on the students' service records.[16] A golf course and the American Legion Club were located in this area following World War II.

Chemical warfare training was another component of the overseas curriculum. A tear gas chamber was constructed and, on a weekly basis, trainees donned gas masks for regular and special alert drills. Some unfortunate students had gas masks that leaked and while in the gas chamber they had a tearful experience.[17]

A basic part of the training for ROM students was learning the principles of concealment. In addition to the camouflaged Covert Training Unit, another camouflage training area was created and trainees underwent a four-hour course. For two hours they listened to lectures and watched training films. The remaining two hours were spent in a "hands on" experience which would be invaluable in the

Tear gas drill—the mask would sometimes leak. *Center for Western Studies.*

preparation of an advance base or if they were forced to parachute into enemy territory.[18]

## OTHER SECURITY UNITS

*Emergency Unit:* Other men, primarily Permanent Party, were selected for special duty. The Provost Marshall had a special security detachment for emergency situations. These men, clad in fatigues, leggings and helmets, drilled every Thursday from 3:00 to 5:00 P.M. They would support the Military Police detachment in crisis situations. The security unit was divided into four squads: rifle squad, sub-machine gun squad, hand grenade squad and a tear gas squad. All of the squads engaged in bayonet drills, necessary for hand-to-hand combat.[19]

*Crash Crew:* The base had a crash crew, also made up of Permanent Party. This unit was trained to fight gasoline fires if a base plane should crash. They learned procedures for quickly extracting air crews who might be trapped in a burning plane. The crew used foam and fog to smother the flames. The foam method involved using chemicals and compressed air to form a mist. The ATS had two crash trucks.[20] The men wore special suits of heavy fireproof cloth.

On their heads, and to protect their faces, they wore a plaster hood similar to a welder's mask.[21]

*Control Tower:* This structure overlooked the flying field and was manned by what the GIs called the aerial traffic cops. By radio and signal light the men in the tower directed all take-offs and landings on the flight line and the airborne traffic of all planes within a three mile control zone. Tower personnel were members of the Army Airways Communication System which maintained similar airdrome traffic control all over the globe.[22]

*Sub-Depot:* Work in the Sub-Depot was divided into three categories: administrative, supply and maintenance. Members of the Signal Corps maintained the magnetic compass, the loop antenna and other radio equipment. Personnel in the Sub-Depot were in charge of the Mae West life jackets. The Parachute and Fabric Department was responsible for the drying, packing and storage of parachutes and sewing jobs on bomb rack curtains, seat covering and wing fabric. The maintenance area also housed the mechanics who ensured that all aircraft were ready for flight and that all base vehicles, such as trucks and Jeeps, were in proper running order.

*Military Police:* The Military Police (MPs) served several functions. Sixteen men were assigned to ride on the Hiawatha and Arrow passenger trains from Sioux Falls to Chicago and return to Sioux Falls. Each man traveled approximately 2,400 miles per week. Their time off was spent resting at the Lorraine Hotel, the MP Battalion Headquarters in Chicago. Eight men were assigned to each train. The MPs preserved order among military personnel and rendered aid and assistance when needed. They watched for gambling, riding on platforms, opening doors, leaning out of windows, drunk and disorderly conduct, damaging equipment, improper seating, slovenly dress and behaving obnoxiously. They also checked furlough papers, passes and tickets. On occasion, they apprehended AWOL personnel and served as military guards.[23]

A staff car and two reconnaissance vehicles were equipped with radio sets that enabled the men on patrol to keep in constant contact with the base Military Police headquarters while patrolling Sioux Falls streets. MPs were also stationed at the headquarters of the city police department and they cooperated in handling drunk and disorderly GIs, breaking up fights between soldiers and checking out night clubs, primarily on West 12th Street in Sioux Falls.

As members of the 929th Guard Squadron, the MPs also rode fence from sundown to sunrise, between 1915 and 0500 (7:15 P.M.-5:00 A.M.). When engaged in fence patrol they had "handie talkies," portable sending and receiving sets, permitting them to keep in constant contact with base headquarters. Battery powered, the sets had a range of one-and-a-half miles.[24] Battery life was approximately fourteen hours.

Thirty men from the 85th Squadron (the African-American Squadron) studied to be MPs. Detached from regular service with the squadron for two weeks, they attended a school for Military Police eight hours a day. They were taught military courtesy, discipline, use of Army Air Forces weapons and the rules and regulations governing MPs. They were assigned to Gates 1, 3 and 4 at the base. Following their assigned shift for the day, they studied the Pass System, Post Regulations and first aid for an hour each day.

*Kitchen Patrol:* Most GIs disliked being assigned to the kitchen where they helped process food (e.g., peeling potatoes, etc.), and adhered to the requests of the cooks for this pan or dish. The most onerous of Kitchen Patrol (KP) duties was cleaning the tables and washing the dishes and pans before the men were dismissed. Upon arriving at their barracks, they looked forward to a shower, especially the men who had worked in the steam and sweat associated with washing dishes, pans and pots.

## VOLUNTEERS FOR THE HARVEST

By the fall of 1942, the military draft was taking its toll on farm labor. A request by Secretary of Agriculture Claude Wickard that soldiers be used to aid farmers with the wheat harvest in South Dakota was vigorously rejected by the War Department.[25] Requests from other Great Plains states prior to the 1943 fall harvest were also rejected by federal officials. Chester Davis, Director of the War Food Administration (WFA), and Paul V. McNutt, Director of the War Mobilization Committee (WMC), proposed the mobilization of a 3.5 million "land army" for seasonal work on farms across the nation. Farmers opposed the proposal referring to such workers as "those back to the soil patriots" and listed several shortcomings indicating that such a program was unrealistic. They argued that such a labor force would be unskilled, that suitable housing was not available and that most farms did not have running water. Thus, they would have to rely on the traditional outhouse.[26]

Farm organizations offered their own proposal. They recommended short-term farm furloughs whereby soldiers would be released from their duties, particularly during the harvest season. Farmers would pay the prevailing wage directly to the Treasury Department while soldiers who volunteered for farm work received their regular pay. In southeast South Dakota, a farmer who needed assistance with either shocking or threshing would contact the base commander for available volunteers. The Army opposed the foregoing procedure but President Franklin Roosevelt liked the plan and approved it in late February 1943.[27]

Interested GIs signed up for the farm labor pool. Colonel Cote and his successor, Colonel Rogers, said the soldiers must do it in their free time. The two commanders insisted that the men would not be released from their base duties. Farmers were required to make arrangements for transporting the soldiers to their farms.[28] The Sioux Falls office of the U.S. Employment Service served as the intermediary between the farmer and the base commander's office.[29]

Sergeant Weller round-raking new-mown hay on a South Dakota farm.
*Center for Western Studies.*

REVEILLE FOR SIOUX FALLS

Clockwise: a radioman learns how a binder functions, break time in the field, a hearty meal at Vincent Leber's farmhouse near Parker, South Dakota, and shocking grain. *Center for Western Studies*.

Approximately 900 GIs, both radio students and Permanent Party, volunteered to work in farm fields on their days off.

In late July 1943, the first contingent of GIs, six of them, went to work on the Vincent Leber farm near Parker, South Dakota. One of the soldiers from Chicago asked what a binder was. The operation of the binder was explained to the GIs. One of the men, a former farmer, drove the tractor while Leber rode the binder. The other volunteers put up shocks in a field that had been cut earlier. Leber and his cohort on the tractor took care of a seventy-acre field in little over a day. The men were paid fifty cents per hour; their earnings were directed to the U.S. Treasury. At the dinner table that evening the GIs enjoyed fried ham, fried chicken, carrots, macaroni salad, potatoes, rice pudding and coffee. Leber commented, "Those fellows are a darned good bunch."[30]

In August 1943, 5,100 GIs from Army installations in seven states were sent to North Dakota to help harvest crops. The Sioux Falls contingent was composed of graduating students who were assigned to this task for physical conditioning prior to overseas service.[31] By mid-1944, the hours volunteers could work in the harvest fields had been increased. They were excused immediately after school on Saturday. Farmers provided board and one night's lodging and paid the soldiers sixty cents an hour, picking them up at Gate 2 and returning the men on Sunday evening before 2200 (10:00 P.M.).[32] Some of the men would return to the base with blisters on their hands.

During the redeployment period at the base, following the German surrender in Western Europe on May 8, 1945, many of the GIs passing through the base volunteered their spare time to work on a farm. Appreciative farmers would ask for the same crew for the following day. Most of the officers and enlisted men had prior farm experience in their home communities. Some who had no experience were eager to learn. There is an account, perhaps apocryphal, that one inexperienced crew, asked to shock at a farm near Flandreau, at first arranged the bundles upside down with the heads on the bottom and the stems on top. Twenty-one men working in the Salem area shocked 200 acres of oats in a day. Approximately 200 farmers in Minnehaha County and adjacent counties had Army personnel help with harvesting and haying operations. Their free nights were a real treat as they sat down in the farm kitchen to a loaded table with no standing in line.[33] Between July 25 and August 3, base personnel worked 8,869 hours on farms in the Sioux Falls area. On the peak day, August 7, 883 men were in the harvest field.

# Chapter 6

*The only bum steer we got here was the propaganda about "dry cold" being easy to take.*
*– Argus Leader, December 9, 1942*

*Sioux Falls is the only place where you can stand knee deep in mud and have the dust blowing in your face at the same time.*
*– Argus Leader, August 24, 1943*

When the Army Air Forces Technical School was constructed in the spring and early summer of 1942, the War Department did not take into consideration that the new school was the northernmost of the technical training centers. Working against a deadline, plus bureaucratic bungling, construction of the living quarters for the enlisted men did not provide adequate protection from South Dakota winters.

## LIVING QUARTERS

One GI, arriving on December 5, 1942, Arthur S. Johnson III, said his first impressions of the Army Technical School were not very good. He wrote, "As far as you could see there were one-story dark brown barracks with black stove pipes poking from the roofs. The ground was hard packed gravel with drainage ditches and culverts, and no sign of greenery anywhere. The brownish smoke pouring from the stove pipes made the air hard to breathe. I tried to take a walk and a run, but it was no fun. The food wasn't especially good either."[1]

The barracks, placed on concrete slabs, were constructed of boards covered with tar paper and lathes. There was no insulation in the walls. Except for the concrete floor and size, the barracks resembled the claim shacks that dotted the Dakota plains in the latter

A soldier navigates the path between the barracks at the technical school.
*Courtesy Arthur S. Johnson.*

part of the nineteenth century or the *stalags* that housed Allied POWs during the war.  The ATS was a temporary camp built to last for about five years.

Only the single-story barracks were about 150 feet long with a door at each end.  The air base had been laid out northwest to southeast.  When contending with prevailing winds, the soldiers soon learned that opening the front door would cause the back door to blow open.  During the winter, what heat the barracks contained would go out the back door.  Later on, as an afterthought, vestibules were built on the front and rear of the barracks.[2]

Using the newly constructed spur track and preparing for the winter of 1942, carloads of coal were brought onto the base during August.  It was estimated that approximately 50,000 tons of coal would be needed to heat the base.  During a six-week period, 1,000 carloads of bituminous (soft) coal arrived at the base at a rate of fifty cars per day.[3]  The coal was unloaded in a storage area adjacent to what was to be the African-American troops' barracks.[4]  The day after he graduated from the Army Technical School, PFC Johnson recalled being assigned to the coal pile. He and other men shoveled five truck loads of over a ton each in the morning and four more in the afternoon. He recalled, "I don't think I had been so dirty since cleaning out the sooty furnaces for Mr. Skillin back in Natick [Massachusetts]."[5]

Each barrack was heated with two or three pot-bellied stoves located in the center aisle of the building. Very few of the men knew how to start and maintain a fire in the stoves, which would often go out during the cold winter nights.[6] Every barrack had posters outlining the proper procedure for firing the stoves. Often, the men ignored these instructions.[7] The posters, entitled "The Care and Feeding of the Hand-Fired Coal Stove," included the following instructions: "As the lid of the stove being hot, it is a temptation to drop it instead of letting it down gently. This can cause cracking of the brittle iron. You must shovel and remove the ashes, keeping the pit clean to prevent burning out the grate." Piling coal to the top of the stove, usually motivated by a reluctance to stoke the blaze frequently had two bad results. It closed the air ports at the sides, destroying the effectiveness of the heating and it put the fire at the top of the stove, causing the intense heat to burn out the sheet metal pipes.[8]

The barracks became notorious for their discomfort. Efforts to maintain a fire throughout the cold winter nights often failed.

Sioux Falls ATS buildings under construction during the muddy spring of 1942. *Center for Western Studies.*

Rear of barracks—more water and mud. *Courtesy Arthur S. Johnson.*

Even though there were assigned firemen for each barracks and for the other buildings, soldiers would more than likely wake up in the morning to discover cold stoves. On occasion, snow would blow into the barracks and it often became so cold that the men could not sleep.[9] The men piled on coats and blankets attempting to keep warm. Francis Mainolfi woke up one morning and saw that the thermometer read eight below zero, and that was inside the barrack.[10] Except for constructing the vestibules, no further steps were taken to combat the cold. Wooden floors in each barrack would have been preferable to setting one's toes down on a freezing, concrete floor in the early dawn.[11] Latrines were located in nearby barracks.

Because of the type of coal used and improper firing of the stoves, the base, at times, looked a little like Pittsburgh when it had steel-making facilities.[12] There were several days when the cloud ceiling was so low that training flights for radio students had to be postponed.[13] Smoke and coal dust hung over the base all of the time during the winter months.[14]  One GI commented, "The camp as usual is heavy with smoke and seems to make one believe that he is not a soldier but very much so a coal miner."[15]  The prevalence of smoke and coal dust created health problems, primarily coal smoke pneumonia.[16]  Private Leroy Aden commented that coal smoke pneumonia put him in the hospital for four weeks.[17]

## THE MEMOIRS OF PFC ARTHUR S. JOHNSON

In his *Memoirs*, PFC Arthur S. Johnson III, includes several references to the weather:

> Our routine was reveille at 4:30 A.M. and outside for roll call.  Often we had roll call inside because it was too cold.  It was dark outside anyway, and the air would have been full of yellow smoke tumbling from the stove pipes as the pot bellies were being stoked up.
>
> Studying in the barracks was difficult; the light was dim, and sitting on my cot, I was either too close or too far away from the pot belly stoves.  Lights were turned off at 9:00 P.M.  Sometimes I had to finish a letter in the latrine when the lights went off.  We didn't see the sun for days and

Gravel streets and concrete sidewalks arrive at last. *Courtesy Arthur S. Johnson*

Temporary home for thirty-three GIs, this barrack is ready for morning inspection. The board walls covered only in tar paper and wooden lathe meant that the buildings were very cold. This barrack had three coal-burning stoves. *Center for Western Studies.*

had some blizzards. One day I saw some very brilliant sun dogs with the sun about ten degrees over the horizon. In spite of the weather we did the obstacle course and some running and marching outside, but we did a lot of our calisthenics in the barracks.

One day in February I noted in my journal that *"it was nice and warm that morning in a cold sort of way."* I meant that it was sunny but the wind was sharp. But it began to snow at noon. The next day I was talking about snow drifts all over the place. As the season moderated we had mud and then dust; from the north one day and from the south the next, with visibility less than 100 yards.[18]

## GRIN AND BEAR IT

Despite the expressed discomfort with porous barracks, ice and snow and outdoor temperatures hovering between zero and twenty degrees above plus thirty-five mile-an-hour winds, GIs maintained a sense of humor. A veteran of two winters at the base said, "If these guys think it's cold now, they should have been around in '42, that was the winter to end all winters. It was so cold we used to trap mice by putting cheese under the thermometer bulb. At night, the mercury dropped

so low it hit the mice on the top of the head and knocked them cold."
There was one soldier who thought the weather was great. He had
been previously stationed in the Aleutian Islands. Another GI, a
native of Austin, Texas, said he "walked out of the barrack one night
and saw all the white stuff covering everything." He let out a yippee
of sheer joy. "I was so happy," he said, "that I started running down
the street to celebrate. Then I fell flat on my face. Snow, I love it."[19]
One GI recalled encountering an officer during the winter of 1944:
"I can't forget the startled look on that officer's face as I stepped off
the walk into a snow-filled ditch and disappeared, my hand still raised
in salute."[20]

*Polar Tech* often printed a Humor Column that was designed to
inform or misinform new arrivals at the Army Technical School. In

To care for the hand-fired coal stove, the soldier was to keep the ash pit clear and carefully handle the cast-iron stove top and fire-brick lining, which could easily be cracked by a poker. *Center for Western Studies.*

depicting Minnesota Avenue, the paper described it as the longest street in the world, especially late at night when you have to get back to the base in a hurry. In winter, when the snow was on the avenue, the newspaper called the North Minnesota Avenue hill the best ski-slide in twenty-two states.[21]

## WORKING IN THE BITTER COLD

The weather during the winter of 1944-45 was comparatively mild when measured against the winters of the previous two years. The winter of 1943 had the longest cold spell of the past three winters.

The flag waves over a cold ATS landscape and against a smoky, gray sky.
*Courtesy Siouxland Heritage Museums.*

A canvas cover shelters mechanics as they repair a plane's engine while a cold January wind blows across the landing strip. *Courtesy Doug Uthe.*

During the frigid spell of January 17-21, the mercury hit a low of minus twenty-four degrees. On February 11-12, the temperature dipped to a minus twenty-three degrees. The lowest reading for the winter of 1944-45 was a minus ten degrees on January 2.[22]

The air base continued to operate in the bitter cold of winter. The GIs' wake-up call came in the misty pre-dawn hours when the entire field was blanketed in silence. During the winter of 1943-44, a soldier wrote home that "We are still plugging along getting up by the light of the moon, racing to the mess hall at 5 in the morning. I assure you, it is quite the thing seeing the moon in all her glory just before the dawn breaks."[23] Mechanics proceeded to put their planes through a series of checks and warm them up ready to fly. The men worked in the teeth of bitter winds howling over the landing strips unhampered by trees or buildings. The back wash of propellers added to the general wind-swept feeling. Snowplows worked the flight line, cleaning runways of snow that accumulated during the night. Lambskin head gear, heavy gloves and extra outer-clothing were a necessity under these circumstances. Fortunate mechanics often worked inside a portable canvas work shed that shielded them from a portion of the cold winds. Throughout the snowy nights, sentries continued to man their posts, firemen made their rounds and MPs walked their assigned routes and stood watch at the post's gates.[24]

## WAITING FOR SPRING

One December evening, with the temperature hovering near zero and chilly blasts sweeping across the air base, a group of enlisted men stood by Gate 2 with hands in their pockets. Driving through the gate, an officer heading into the city stopped his car to remind the men that having their hands in their pockets was against regulations. Not wanting to be too severe in his reprimand, he opened the door and asked the men if they were cold. Before he could say another word, five GIs hopped in his car, thanking him profusely for what they thought was a proffered ride. The officer later remarked, "What could I do. I took them where they were going and forgot about the lecture."[25]

For many of the soldiers who had never experienced a winter on the Northern Plains, spring could not come too soon. They would retain memories of snow drifts piled high against the barracks, often up to the windows.[26] Men looked forward to spending time in the city, not only to socialize but to find a place where they could keep warm.[27]

With temperatures below the freezing mark, the base commander ordered soldiers to wear either lambskin or cloth head gear. Many of the men preferred their olive-drab (OD) garrison caps as they looked more stylish. This obeisance to vanity, however, had caused too many cases of frostbite and frozen ears. Medical doctors in the dispensary noted that after the new order went into effect, they had not had a single patient with either frostbite or frozen ears. In contending with the elements, the men wore heavy winter coats, woolen underwear, gloves and blouses.[28] Colonel Narcisse L. Cote, the base commander during 1942-43, even required the men to wear four buckle overshoes when going off base. After passing through Gate 2, the GIs found places to store their overshoes before taking to the streets of Sioux Falls, and MPs tended to overlook this violation of an OD order.[29]

Naturally, the men became impatient for the arrival of spring. They dreamed of boating on Covell Lake, outdoor dances, picnics and baseball. A South Dakota winter, however, does not easily loosen its grip. For example, on March 28, 1945, sun-tan uniforms were optional when not in formation. The same day winter returned with a four-hour snowstorm and the temperature dipping to thirty-four degrees.[30] In early April 1945, there was still much snow on the ground. The *Polar Tech* featured a picture faking baseball practice in the snow.[31] Continuing in a humorous vein, the newspaper, on May 18, 1945, made several recommendations for equipment for the spring weather: "Fog lights to be worn by distance runners, baseball bats with built-in umbrellas, steam heated players' benches, specially weighted shoes to keep outfielders from blowing away, and heated track suits complete with fur-lined hoods and boots with a special attachment for snow shoes."[32] A welcome sight appeared a week later—storm windows were being removed from the barracks.[33] The weather remained cool well into June 1945. OD clothing had been optional. At this time, in any other year, khaki would have been the official dress.[34]

## WHAT IS THE UNIFORM OF THE DAY?

Sudden changes in the weather caused problems when prescribing the uniform of the day. Early one morning, during the last week of March 1943, Colonel N. L. Cote prescribed the uniform of the day based on a weather report he received at 4:00 A.M. He ordered the men to wear knit caps and overcoats. Sioux Falls experienced a heat wave that day as the temperature reached eighty-two degrees. With the intense heat, GIs on day leave in the city removed the forenamed items of clothing. The military police picked up more than 250 ATS soldiers on the streets and returned them to the base for not appearing in proper uniform. No disciplinary action was taken against them.[35]

In mid-May 1943, the men were told to make certain that they had two sets of khakis, replacing their olive-drab uniforms. They were huddled in their overcoats when this order came. They immediately made plans to wear long underwear under the khakis.[36]

In April 1945, there was snow on the ground until the middle of the month. Soon after they adapted to their sun-tan uniforms, there was a sudden return of winter with a several hour snowstorm in early

May and the temperature falling to the low thirties. Chilly weather continued on into June causing the base commander to make the uniform of the day optional.[37]

## HEAT AND DUST

Most of the men complained about the cold, but several soldiers had difficulty adjusting to the summer heat and wind-blown dust. Ken Berry, an instructor from New England, said the plains seemed strange. He commented that he froze in the winter and baked in the summer in the barracks.[38] Several of the newly arrived GIs suffered from severe prickly heat and were admitted to the hospital.[39] As noted above, Arthur Johnson kept a daily journal while stationed at the base from December 1942 to May 1943. He was also from New England, and many of his journal entries describe the weather. When arriving by train at the ATS on December 5, 1942, Johnson wrote, "These towns aren't very wonderful looking. Lot of small, dumpy houses. Lots of dirt roads in town. Don't look very prosperous." Other entries include the following:

December 13, 1942 – "Went to No. 4 for lunch, was sent to No. 5, sent back to the barracks. Finally back to No. 5 for mess. Boy, is it cold."

January 16, 1943 – "Today is two months in the Army. How many more? Started in on Receivers. Hooked up a detector stage and heard KSOO. Some fun! Good-sized blizzard today. Cold, strong wind. Snow drifts all over. Saw two vertical sun dogs about 15 to 20 degrees either side of the sun that was about 10 degrees above the horizon."

February 5 – "This makes two months at this wretched place in South Dakota."

February 16 – "Passed 14 wpm. Had to fight for it. Had a nice long hike. Weather has moderated but it freezes every night without fail."

March 16 – "What a day! Snow, high winds. You can hardly stand up. Cold, too. Boy that wind is really blowing. The snow doesn't stay anywhere. This after the icy surfaces from the rain yesterday."

April 5 – "The weather was okay when we got up, but around the middle of the morning it began to blow from the south, hard, kicking

g from the scene told others that
og tags."

oted by Willard Woody of North
lls. With one engine on fire, he
itude for forty minutes. During
P. Galen, Texola, Oklahoma, and
E. Vandkirk, Sioux Center, Iowa,
tudents. They gave the students
ull the rip cord and then shoved
dy was the last to jump from the
s only 700 feet above the ground.
e would have failed to save him.[49]
ing used as Flying Classrooms.
ssigned to fly the planes.[50] Each
nstructors. Every trainee was to
, with a plan in place to increase

topic of conversation, was no
t the Sioux Falls Army Technical
e prolonged winter cold and the
e at the base hospital with coal
r that instigated construction of
nd it was adverse weather that
mber 8, 1944.

lied as a result of the mid-air
srooms" on December 8, 1944,

ey, 23, Massachusetts

mes D. Simmons, 26, Illinois

llman, 21, Ohio

uisiana

8, Tennessee

up the dust! Wow! I have never seen anything like it. The damn stuff gets in everywhere."

April 29 – [Day following graduation] "What a day! Nuts to Sioux Falls!"[40]

## A NEW SWIMMING POOL

By mid-July 1942, with temperatures in the mid-nineties, ATS personnel, if off duty, joined the civilian population at an overcrowded Drake Springs swimming pool.[41] Desiring to avoid the continued congestion at the city's one swimming pool, ATS personnel, with the approval of the base commander, began the construction of a new swimming pool adjacent to Covell Lake in late 1943. Construction of the Terrace Park pool continued through the winter and early spring of 1944. Many nights, the men who volunteered to construct the new pool, worked long hours after their regular duty hours. They stayed on the job regardless of weather conditions. In mid-winter, the temperature dropped to twenty degrees below zero but they continued with their work. They poured concrete long after their duty hours had come to an end.[42] The new pool was expected to be ready for use by Memorial Day 1944. By April 28, work on the pool itself was complete; the filter house was ready with the exception of plumbing facilities.[43] The new pool measured 100' x 200' and ranged in depth from 3.5' to 11.5'. It was almost equal in size to that of Drake Springs. Diving towers, spring boards and other accessories were added later. The official opening of the Terrace Park pool did not take place until the last week in June because of a leak.

The new pool was to be used primarily for the physical training needs of military personnel. Recreational swimming was permitted at specified times during the day. Soldiers stationed at the base were permitted to have civilian guests after Army demands were met.[44]

## TRAINING FLIGHTS AND DISASTER

The radio trainees engaged in course work for five to ten months. For the first eighteen months, the final exam was conducted in the fuselage of a scrapped B-25 bomber. After that time, students took their final exam in a plane in flight. If the student passed, he was usually transferred to gunnery school before being assigned as a radio operator-mechanic to battle duty aboard medium and heavy bombers where he would send and receive messages in code.[45]

The Army Technical School first used Lockheed Hudson twin engine AT-18 medium bombers as "flying classrooms." The interiors of these dull silver-gray aircraft had been stripped and replaced with tables and radio equipment to provide students with actual flight training. One minor problem with these planes was the gas tank on the wing. It was metal against metal sealed with an adhesive compound. Pilots soon learned that if they landed hard they would jar the seam and gas would leak out of the tank. Planes experiencing this problem were red-lined for two days while the seams were repaired.[46]

Cruising at 190 miles per hour, the AT-18s would fly from Sioux Falls to Lafayette, Minnesota (north of New Ulm), then turn west and fly over Bruce, South Dakota, before returning to Sioux Falls. The flight usually took no more than three hours. For twenty-nine months, the base never had a fatal flying accident after almost 50,000 hours of flight training. As noted earlier, three soldiers stationed at the base had been killed in automobile and motorcycle accidents.[47]

The no-crash record ended suddenly on December 8, 1944. Adverse weather conditions that day permitted the flight of only two AT-18s. The sky was overcast with a low, dense cloud ceiling. Sleet and snow combined with fog made it difficult to pick out the outline of a silver-gray plane in the pea-soup air. The two airborne planes crossed flight patterns resulting in the mid-air collision. One plane, piloted by First Lieutenant Paul Currey, was attempting to land, the other had just taken off. They collided at an estimated 1,500 feet above the air field.

It was shortly before 3:00 P.M. when witnesses observed one of the AT-18s rocketing out of a cloud bank at high speed and clipping the tail assembly of the plane that had just taken off. One of the disabled craft veered into a flat spin, spiraling into a free fall, littering the training field with tail parts. The falling AT-18 veered toward the enlisted men's barracks. It tore through thick, high tension wires cutting power and communication lines. Electric clocks on the base stopped at 2:59 P.M.

Unless they were in class, soldiers were spending the day lounging in their barracks. The plane plowed into the front door of Squadron P barrack and exploded into flames. One unhappy trainee, because he had wanted to fly that day, had his bunk just inside the front door

the building.[48] An officer returning "There was nothing left but their de

The other damaged plane, pil Carolina, flew north from Sioux Fa was able to maintain satisfactory al this time, his crew chief, PFC Alex radio instructor Sergeant Johannes checked the parachutes of the six s instructions on when and how to p each student out of the plane. Woo aircraft. He left the plane when it wa Two hundred feet lower and his chu

A month later, C-47s were be Fifteen former combat pilots were a plane carried ten students and two have at least six hours of flying time the number to twelve.[51]

The weather, always a favorit exception among the men stationed School. They always remembered th hot summers. Many men spent tim dust pneumonia. It was the weathe the Terrace Park swimming pool, a caused the fatal plane crash on Dece

The ten young airmen who d collision of two AT-18 "Flying Clas were the following:

Crew:

First Lieutenant Paul S. Curr

Crew Chief, Staff Sergeant Ja

Instructor, PFC Orville J. Spe

Students:

Private Floyd R. Terral, 24, L

Private Edward M. Gregory,

up the dust! Wow! I have never seen anything like it. The damn stuff gets in everywhere."

April 29 – [Day following graduation] "What a day! Nuts to Sioux Falls!"[40]

## A NEW SWIMMING POOL

By mid-July 1942, with temperatures in the mid-nineties, ATS personnel, if off duty, joined the civilian population at an overcrowded Drake Springs swimming pool.[41] Desiring to avoid the continued congestion at the city's one swimming pool, ATS personnel, with the approval of the base commander, began the construction of a new swimming pool adjacent to Covell Lake in late 1943. Construction of the Terrace Park pool continued through the winter and early spring of 1944. Many nights, the men who volunteered to construct the new pool, worked long hours after their regular duty hours. They stayed on the job regardless of weather conditions. In mid-winter, the temperature dropped to twenty degrees below zero but they continued with their work. They poured concrete long after their duty hours had come to an end.[42] The new pool was expected to be ready for use by Memorial Day 1944. By April 28, work on the pool itself was complete; the filter house was ready with the exception of plumbing facilities.[43] The new pool measured 100' x 200' and ranged in depth from 3.5' to 11.5'. It was almost equal in size to that of Drake Springs. Diving towers, spring boards and other accessories were added later. The official opening of the Terrace Park pool did not take place until the last week in June because of a leak.

The new pool was to be used primarily for the physical training needs of military personnel. Recreational swimming was permitted at specified times during the day. Soldiers stationed at the base were permitted to have civilian guests after Army demands were met.[44]

## TRAINING FLIGHTS AND DISASTER

The radio trainees engaged in course work for five to ten months. For the first eighteen months, the final exam was conducted in the fuselage of a scrapped B-25 bomber. After that time, students took their final exam in a plane in flight. If the student passed, he was usually transferred to gunnery school before being assigned as a radio operator-mechanic to battle duty aboard medium and heavy bombers where he would send and receive messages in code.[45]

The Army Technical School first used Lockheed Hudson twin-engine AT-18 medium bombers as "flying classrooms." The interiors of these dull silver-gray aircraft had been stripped and replaced with tables and radio equipment to provide students with actual flight training. One minor problem with these planes was the gas tank on the wing. It was metal against metal sealed with an adhesive compound. Pilots soon learned that if they landed hard they would jar the seams and gas would leak out of the tank. Planes experiencing this problem were red-lined for two days while the seams were repaired.[46]

Cruising at 190 miles per hour, the AT-18s would fly from Sioux Falls to Lafayette, Minnesota (north of New Ulm), then turn west and fly over Bruce, South Dakota, before returning to Sioux Falls. The flight usually took no more than three hours. For twenty-nine months, the base never had a fatal flying accident after almost 50,000 hours of flight training. As noted earlier, three soldiers stationed at the base had been killed in automobile and motorcycle accidents.[47]

The no-crash record ended suddenly on December 8, 1944. Adverse weather conditions that day permitted the flight of only two AT-18s. The sky was overcast with a low, dense cloud ceiling. Sleet and snow combined with fog made it difficult to pick out the outline of a silver-gray plane in the pea-soup air. The two airborne planes crossed flight patterns resulting in the mid-air collision. One plane, piloted by First Lieutenant Paul Currey, was attempting to land, the other had just taken off. They collided at an estimated 1,500 feet above the air field.

It was shortly before 3:00 P.M. when witnesses observed one of the AT-18s rocketing out of a cloud bank at high speed and clipping the tail assembly of the plane that had just taken off. One of the disabled craft veered into a flat spin, spiraling into a free fall, littering the training field with tail parts. The falling AT-18 veered toward the enlisted men's barracks. It tore through thick, high tension wires, cutting power and communication lines. Electric clocks on the base stopped at 2:59 P.M.

Unless they were in class, soldiers were spending the day lounging in their barracks. The plane plowed into the front door of Squadron P barrack and exploded into flames. One unhappy trainee, because he had wanted to fly that day, had his bunk just inside the front door.

When the plane hit the barrack, the two engines dug into the ground on both sides of the door. The wings sheared through the building and right through the trainee.

Prior to the crash, three area men had been in the barrack. They were Robert Lindblad of Huron and Robert Callies and Harold Wingler of Sioux Falls. Upon hearing the sound of the plane's engines coming ever closer, Lindblad and Callies, both nineteen, and another man raced to the back door. Callies, who had been changing clothes, raced away from death and out into the December cold wearing only a pair of pants and a shirt. As he ran for the back door, he thought the plane was going to hit him in the head. One other man who chose to race toward the front door was killed. Prior to the plane's impact, twenty-four-year-old Sergeant Wingler had walked out the front door after telling the approximately half-dozen men to fall-out for physical training. He was temporarily mesmerized by the approaching aircraft. He could see the faces of the pilot and crew chief behind the Plexi-glas shield in front of the cockpit. He quickly recovered from his trance-like state and ran about 100 feet before the force of the plane's contact with the barrack and the ground knocked him down. The concussion from the plane's impact also flattened Callies and Lindblad. Lindblad got up and started running. He did not stop until he reached the base's main gate three city blocks away. One of the men remaining in the barrack had crawled out of a window but he crawled toward the oncoming plane. Wingler surmised that the man had lost his sense of direction or that he was attempting to help members of the crew still trapped in their seats in the burning plane. The soldier was killed in the ensuing explosion.

The base fire crew battled the blaze but before it was quelled two adjoining barracks also burned. As the plane burned, scores of GIs scrambled to the roofs of adjoining barracks either to get a good view or camera-shot of the scene. An enraged base commander, Colonel Oscar L. Rogers, scurried around, yanking cameras away from the enlisted men and smashing them with his boots. He considered any information or photographs of the crash to be classified information. The only picture to appear in the *Argus Leader* was of the charred remains of the plane and the barracks. *Polar Tech* briefly noted the accident. All seven men aboard the plane perished in their seats. The two men in the barrack were killed as well as the one soldier outside the building.[48]  An officer returning from the scene told others that "There was nothing left but their dog tags."

The other damaged plane, piloted by Willard Woody of North Carolina, flew north from Sioux Falls.  With one engine on fire, he was able to maintain satisfactory altitude for forty minutes.  During this time, his crew chief, PFC Alex P. Galen, Texola, Oklahoma, and radio instructor Sergeant Johannes E. Vandkirk, Sioux Center, Iowa, checked the parachutes of the six students.  They gave the students instructions on when and how to pull the rip cord and then shoved each student out of the plane.  Woody was the last to jump from the aircraft.  He left the plane when it was only 700 feet above the ground.  Two hundred feet lower and his chute would have failed to save him.[49]

A month later, C-47s were being used as Flying Classrooms.  Fifteen former combat pilots were assigned to fly the planes.[50]  Each plane carried ten students and two instructors.  Every trainee was to have at least six hours of flying time, with a plan in place to increase the number to twelve.[51]

The weather, always a favorite topic of conversation, was no exception among the men stationed at the Sioux Falls Army Technical School.  They always remembered the prolonged winter cold and the hot summers.  Many men spent time at the base hospital with coal dust pneumonia.  It was the weather that instigated construction of the Terrace Park swimming pool, and it was adverse weather that caused the fatal plane crash on December 8, 1944.

The ten young airmen who died as a result of the mid-air collision of two AT-18 "Flying Classrooms" on December 8, 1944, were the following:

Crew:

First Lieutenant Paul S. Currey, 23, Massachusetts

Crew Chief, Staff Sergeant James D. Simmons, 26, Illinois

Instructor, PFC Orville J. Spellman, 21, Ohio

Students:

Private Floyd R. Terral, 24, Louisiana

Private Edward M. Gregory, 18, Tennessee

The Raiders African-American baseball team of Section F. In the second row (l to r) is T/Sgt. Olin "Jelly" Taylor, the manager, wearing a Memphis Red Sox shirt. At the end of the second row is Captain J. E. Shannon, commander of Section F. In the top row, second from the right, is Pvt. Riley Stewart, who played a significant role in the integration of baseball. *Center for Western Studies*.

Paige, a legendary black pitcher. Taylor had a lifetime batting average of .302 and a fielding average of better than .980.

In 1945, the Raiders won the Little Sioux League title when they defeated their yearly nemesis, the ATS Marauders, a white team. The other four teams in the league were the Morrell Packers, Al's Place, Ellis and the Mint Bar. "Jelly" Taylor was the pitcher and the hitting star as he had five consecutive hits in one game.[31] Riley Stewart played a significant role in the first integration of baseball. He was a part of the Marauders squad during the Semi-Pro Baseball Congress in Wichita, Kansas. The Marauders, having defeated Williams Field, Arizona, 2-0 and Camp Chaffee, Arkansas, 3-2 had Stewart on the mound as they pursued a third-round victory. He was brilliant through eight innings.[32] Stewart went on to play minor league baseball after the war, including a stint with the Brookings, South Dakota, amateur baseball team.[33]

In July 1945, Jesse Owens visited the base. He challenged two black soldiers to race against him at Howard Wood Field. Private Ervine Campbell and Private First Class Riley Stewart from Squadron C accepted the challenge. It had been nine years since his triumph at the 1936 Olympics in Berlin, Germany, but Owens won the race.[34] The 85th Aviation Squadron moved into its own gymnasium in February 1944, located in the Squadron's area. Activities at this sports arena included boxing, basketball, wrestling and several other indoor sports.[35]

The African-American soldiers from the Deep South were always concerned about the people of their race back home. During the Christmas season of 1942, members of the 85th Aviation Squadron raised $1,227.50 to provide gifts for underprivileged children in the South. The check was sent to President A.D. Patterson of Tuskegee Institute, Tuskegee, Alabama. They were responding to a plea from Patterson who had written a letter to the editor of *Polar Tech* asking for gifts to alleviate poor family conditions due to wartime manpower dislocation. The collection that was taken up after the monthly pay day averaged $5.00 per man.[36]

During that same Christmas season, there appeared a disconcerting article in the December 12 issue of *Business Week.* The article supposedly assessed conditions in communities adjacent to army camps. Regarding Sioux Falls, the article stated, "Sioux Falls, South Dakota was a trouble center. There an Army Air Forces technical training field suffered numerous racial difficulties. Personnel consisted of thousands of white men, many from the South, and

The Raiders baseball team in front of their dugout at the ATS. *Center for Western Studies.*

Jesse Owens, a 1936 Olympic Champion (center), races against two of the base's fastest runners—Pvt. Irvine Campbell and PFC Riley Stewart. Owens won before a crowd of 3,500 fans. *Center for Western Studies.*

about 300 northern Negroes.  Whites and blacks relaxed in the same saloons and fights became alarmingly frequent."[37]

The editor of the *Argus Leader* issued a rebuttal.  He stated that the difficulties described in *Business Week* were a product of some writer's fertile imagination.  He said it was not even remotely accurate. The editor was correct—there had been no trouble of consequence.[38] Bessie Vaughn, wife of Theodore Vaughn, who had been stationed at the base, said there had been no serious trouble.[39]  Paul Graves, one of the first soldiers to arrive at the ATS as an instructor, and an acute observer of base activities, stated there were no problems with the black squadron. He viewed it as a quiet operation.[40]  The writer's statement that there were about 300 northern Negroes at the base is a further indication of false journalism.  A majority of the black soldiers at the ATS were from the South, in particular Alabama and Georgia. Prentiss L. Pemberton, in a letter to the editor of the *Argus Leader*, summed it up quite well: "While we still encounter problems of discrimination, the intelligent leadership of public-spirited citizens has formulated here a colored policy generally progressive." He urged Sioux Falls to continue its progress towards total elimination of racial discrimination.  Pemberton concluded by stating, "Appreciating the remarkable cultural advances already achieved by our colored people against almost insurmountable obstacles, let our intelligence and

The three ATS boxing champions preparing for the Sioux City Golden Glove Tournament. *Center for Western Studies.*

understanding speed that advance with the least possible tension and conflict."[41]

## NEW BEGINNINGS

Following their discharge from military service after the war ended, the majority of the African-American soldiers returned to their pre-war homes. Others moved on to Minneapolis, Sioux City and Waterloo, Iowa. Between fifteen and twenty men returned to Sioux Falls with their families. Their numbers included Jack Armstrong, William Harris, Johnnie Hildreth, Carl Nichols, Charles Smith, Theodore Vaughn and Booker Walker. Hildreth commented that Sioux Falls "was a pretty nice little town to live in and educate our kids." Hildreth spent twenty years as a chef at the Veterans Administration Hospital before starting on his own in the restaurant business. Nichols worked in construction, finishing concrete. Armstrong operated his own paint and body shop. Smith began a cleaning service. Despite the discriminatory treatment they received at the Army Technical School, these men came to enjoy life in their adopted hometown.

There is no doubt that the African-American soldiers received better treatment in the Sioux Falls community than they experienced at the Army Technical School. The base commander's adherence to Army regulations regarding segregation is even found in what might be called the school annuals for graduating classes. The books include many pictures of buildings and activities at the Army Technical School, but no picture of an African–American appears on any of the pages of the first editions.[42]

A radical change occurred shortly after World War II, when President Harry Truman ordered the racial integration of the armed forces. Speaking in a philosophical vein, Armstrong said that attempting integration by force would never work: "You can't work on laws to bring about change. Let's work on individuals in the important place, their hearts. If we do that, we'll come together better as human beings."[43]

# Chapter 8

*If the guys can take it, so can I.*
*– A woman volunteer*

Marjorie Hummel, with a State Teachers Certificate from Columbus Normal School, taught in several schools in Minnehaha County with a starting salary of $540 per year prior to American entry into World War II. When the Sioux Falls Army Technical School opened in July 1942, Marjorie applied for a job teaching future radio operators the Morse code, a position she held until 1945.

Between 1942 and 1945, approximately 1,800 local citizens were employed at the ATS. A significant number of these employees were women. For many of them it was their first job outside of the home. Like Marjorie, they took advantage of the economic opportunities born of the war. They liked the freedom, independence and money. Through their efforts, they made a major contribution to household income. At the same time, work at the air base was synonymous with patriotism and participation in the war effort.

From the time the base opened, the commander, Colonel Narcisse L. Cote, sought civilian instructors for the Instruction Training Division.[1] Among the first women to respond to the call were Mrs. John Whitt and Betty Hervig, a science teacher and the daughter of the Minnehaha County Superintendent of Schools, Edgar Hervig.[2] By midday, July 21, twenty-five women and men had been hired to teach the Morse code and some of the fundamentals of radio operation and maintenance to men who, if they passed the course, would become radio men aboard B-17 and B-24 bombers. Sources indicate that the Sioux Falls Army Technical School was the first to employ women instructors.[3] The twenty-five civilians began attending a three-month training course. If they successfully completed their training, they were to be paid $1,620 per year. Soon thereafter, their wage was raised to $2,000 per year. Opportunities for advancement in position and salary were available.[4]

Female instructors were not permitted to wear slacks at the ATS. Femininity on the base prevailed for instructors. If they went downtown to shop, however, they usually dressed in slacks.[5] The women had various reactions to their work. Edith Cannan remarked that "My special memory is being on three different shifts and trying to get your life adjusted."[6] Sylvia Ekeland Whitt said she had "Many happy memories of teaching some very fine young men." Many of her students were college graduates; a good number had begun professional careers. A large percentage of the men had "washed out" of pilot training.[7]

The students appreciated their female instructors. In January 1943, they established the "Queen of Instructors" contest. A ballot was displayed on the front page of *Polar Tech*. The soldiers were to consider the nominated candidates' ability, personality and popularity. All of the proceeds from the contest went into a Recreation Fund to finance school morale activities.[8]

Several female pilots belonged to an auxiliary organization that transported smaller aircraft from one base to another. *Courtesy Doug Uthe.*

The base motor pool also attracted several civilian women. Lois Johnsrud, a teenager, participated in the motor pool for a short period of time. She transported soldiers around the base and in Sioux Falls. When she told her father it was great fun, he responded, "No more driving for you." She would continue to work at the base but with her mother in the laundry.[9]

Women drivers completed a ten-day training course. Fourteen of the women had completed class work by mid-November 1942. Most of them completed the course with a grade of ninety or better. Their presence released a number of GIs for other duties. The women drove staff cars, half-ton pickups, trucks and carry-all and reconnaissance cars. They were expected to care for their vehicles as had their male predecessors, including changing tires. There were two exceptions: they did not wash or grease their vehicles. Most of the female drivers were assigned to permanent runs but a few were available for general service from the "driver pool."[10] The women wore uniforms and it was a proud day, in April 1943, when they received shoulder patches. The patches were about the size of the Army Air Forces patch. They believed that they were the first female drivers to wear them at any U.S. Army post.[11]

Mary Graves was one of the first ten women employed as a truck driver at the Army Technical School. After two years of college, she had become a rural school teacher, making $75 per month teaching students in grades 1-8. As a twenty-year old truck driver, she made a minimum of $150 per month. As a truck driver, she met Staff Sergeant Paul Graves. They were married in 1944. Mary soon decided she could make more money working as a mechanic on the flight line, first as a welder. As described earlier, the ATA-18 training planes had a major flaw. They had a gas tank sealed to the wing and if a pilot made a hard landing, the jarring opened seams in the tank, causing fuel to leak from the plane. The planes were redlined and not flown again for two days. Mary Graves was one of the welders who closed the open seams. The Air Force preferred women welders because, as in sewing a seam, they made smooth welds. One could hardly discern where the break or breaks on the tank had occurred.

Later, Mary became an assistant to the painter on the flight line. It was her task to paint signs, structural instructions, on the planes. She left the flight line and was assigned to an office in the base laundry. She worked there until 1945 when GIs began to arrive to

Local women who served as drivers for various departments receive their uniforms. The members of the motor pool seen here are the following: Row 1 (l to r) Irene Hylland, Rose Zingleman, Evelyn Westra, Marjory Brekke, Melbo Roll, Eltabel Fenner, Ester Collins, and Mildred Rishoi. Row 2 (l to r) Eunice Hurd, Orene Johnson, Marjorie Wikle, Marilla Butler, Mary Tinkham, Evelyn Palmer, Frances Kenny, Audrey Pedigo, and Ruth Wood. *Center for Western Studies.*

be discharged from military service. Mary then conducted interviews with the men and recorded their wartime experiences. She left the air base in 1945 satisfied that she had done several jobs that had been exclusively men's work prior to World War II.[12]

The laundry had been established in 1943. GIs could use its services for $1.50 per month. Women from Sioux Falls were employed to iron shirts for the men. They also used a "legger" board, which was shaped like a pair of pants. The "legger" eliminated turning the pants over when ironing and it put a sharp crease in a soldier's pants.

Other civilian women worked at the message center at the ATS. One of these women was Judee Koplow. Her mother had worked at the Main Avenue USO. While there, she had observed a young supply sergeant at several dances. Like many Jewish residents, the Koplows invited a few soldiers to come to their home for Friday dinner. The supply sergeant, Sidney Epstein, who had arrived at the Army Technical School in 1942, received an invitation to dinner. When he arrived at the Koplow residence, Judee's mother told her, "That's the guy that used to dance [at the USO] and I want you to meet him." Judee and Sid began dating and they became unofficially engaged at the base hospital while Sid was shaking off the effects of ether following an operation.

They were eventually married in New Jersey when Sid was on furlough. After the war, Sid had planned to return to New Jersey to work in the family's hardware business along with Judee. "She kept putting me off," Sid later related. "Her father owned Koplow Brothers liquor [store]. They put me to work and that's how I got into the liquor business." Sid's Crown Liquor became one of Sioux Falls' longest operating businesses.[13]

S/Sgt. Sidney Epstein in his base office. He married a Sioux Falls girl and later owned and operated a well-known and successful liquor store in Sioux Falls for several decades. *Courtesy Jim Carlson.*

REVEILLE FOR SIOUX FALLS

## MARITAL STATISTICS AS OF JULY 21, 1944

On July 21, 1944, at least 355 GIs, representing all but six states, had taken local women as brides. The following are the states with the most GIs who married women from Sioux Falls:

| | | | |
|---|---|---|---|
| Illinois | 39 | Minnesota | 20 |
| New York | 32 | Texas | 20 |
| Pennsylvania | 30 | Ohio | 19 |
| California | 39 | Wisconsin | 19 |
| | | Missouri | 17[14] |

Women from Sioux Falls also played a significant role at the Army Air Forces hospital. The purpose of the hospital was to restore the health of military personnel as rapidly as possible. This goal was dependent on the work of the medical officers, nurses, dietitians, physical therapists, and the full cooperation of the patients, plus the Gray Ladies from the community.[15]

The Red Cross Gray Lady Corps of the Station Hospital was the first to be organized in South Dakota. Mrs. Zelda Krueger, Secretary of the Minnehaha County Chapter of the Red Cross, directed the Corps' establishment. Mrs. Henry C. Mundt was chairperson of the Gray Lady Corps or the Hospital and Recreation Corps of the Red Cross. They were a group of approximately fifty-five volunteers who provided friendly and helpful services for the sick and convalescent at the hospital. They wore gray uniforms, thus giving them the title Gray Ladies.

To qualify for the Gray Lady Corps, an applicant took a fifteen-hour lecture course followed by twenty-four hours of probationary work. Each woman served a certain number of hours each week at the hospital.[16] The Gray Ladies were organized into committees. They performed several special services of a non-medical nature, such as assisting with entertainment, arranging parties and shopping for the bed ridden. They helped patients with letter writing, providing instructions for arts and crafts and distributing books to ward patients. They composed a hospital newspaper called *Ward-O-Scope*, edited by Mrs. W. E. Grimes. On Mother's Day, they distributed flowers to every young man in the hospital. During the summer, the Gray Ladies kept flowers in the wards and Red Cross rooms.[17]

Rug-making at the hospital became popular with the patients, who found rug-making an absorbing diversion. One soldier made fourteen rugs. The Gray Ladies had to scour downtown stores to find enough cotton yarn to meet demand.[18] The women also assisted with the distribution of meals to the bed-bound patients, including the Station Hospital on Thanksgiving Day. The patients received an abundance of traditional foods, as is seen in this dinner menu for November 25, 1943:

Cream of celery soup and shrimp cocktail

Roasted young Tom turkey, sage dressing and giblet gravy

Whipped potatoes, candied sweet potatoes, baked squash and fresh frozen peas

Head lettuce with Russian dressing, cranberry-orange relish, olives, pickles and celery hearts

Butter-crust rolls, mince and pumpkin pie, fruit cake

Ice cream, assorted fruit, mixed nuts, and hard candy

Cigarettes, cigars and coffee.[19]

The Sioux Valley Camp and Hospital Council purchased a small piano, enabling soldiers in the wards to sing. Earlier, the Council put a baby grand piano in the Army hospital recreation room. Music sped convalescence. The Council also purchased a large phonograph, radio, bass drum, traps and a small snare drum.[20]

Women engaged in several other occupations and recreational activities. Four months after the base opened, there were two women barbers cutting hair in one of the post's barber shops.[21] As noted earlier, Mrs. C. B. Goodrich, a Civilian Defense appointee, enlisted the aid of approximately 350 "Personality Girls." They were to help entertain the men at picnics, parties and dances. A personal interview with each girl was required as Mrs. Goodrich "wanted girls from every walk of life, just as long as their character is irreproachable." The girls were to be strictly regulated. They were required to wear sweaters and skirts at parties.[22] A roster of 250 of these girls was assembled and bonded together in an organization followed by an election of officers. They were to give up many evenings to serve as partners for the GIs. They were given large yellow passes with name plates that gave them access to the base. As they observed their anniversary in August 1944, an average of 135 girls had come to the base for dances. The girls had attended at least one dance a week, paying their own expenses for the commute between their homes and the ATS base.[23]

## WOMEN IN THE MILITARY

The base had its own women in white. They belonged to the National Association of Air Force Women and they were affiliated with the Red Cross. The club was composed of the wives of officers and enlisted men. The wife of the base commander was customarily the president of the club (i.e., in 1944, Mrs. O. L. Rogers, the wife of Colonel Oscar Rogers). They made 1,500 surgical dressings per week, knitted small garments and did mending for the GIs.[24]

The Army Nurse roster at the Station Hospital represented twenty states.[25] The hospital had an adequate supply of nurses until D-Day, June 6, 1944, and during the ensuing months when U. S. forces engaged in bitter battles with the Germans in the Battle of the Bulge and the Hurtgen Forest in Belgium and northeastern France. The need for nurses at the overseas fighting fronts decreased the base's hospital staff to an all-time minimum. At the same time, there was a shortage of trained nurses stateside. Throughout the wards and clinic of the hospital, nurses worked a triple shift around the clock.[26]

When Victory over Japan Day (VJ) finally arrived, the Army Air Forces began to consolidate patients at regional hospitals. At the end of November 1945, the ATS hospital had only eighty-five patients and at the end of the year, the hospital was closed.[27]

As of May 15, 1942, women began to enlist for non-combat duties in the Women's Auxiliary Army Corps (WAAC). Prior to 1943, the only WAACs to appear at the Sioux Falls ATS were there for social reasons. Some social problems had arisen at the base after the all-black 85th Aviation Squadron and the 929th Quartermaster Platoon arrived in Sioux Falls. They were commanded by a white Texan, Captain J. E. Shannon, until the war's end. Recognizing that a problem existed, Colonel Cote formed an agreement with the commander of the Fort Des Moines army base. There was a large contingent of black WAACs at the Iowa base. It was agreed that on one weekend bus loads of WAACs from Fort Des Moines would be bused to Sioux Falls to dance with the black soldiers. In the following week, black soldiers at the ATS, if they were on good behavior, would be bused to Des Moines for dancing and other social activities. The procedure, under strict guidance, worked quite well.[28]

Shortly after the first of the year 1943, Colonel Cote received word that a contingent of WAACs would soon be stationed at the Sioux Falls base. This called for additional construction and by mid-March, barracks for the incoming WAACs were nearly completed. One officer and two auxiliaries arrived to inspect the new facilities. They also opened a WAAC recruiting office in the Sioux Falls Federal Building.[29] Fourteen women, under the command of Lieutenant Jean Cromwell, were in the detachment that arrived on June 11, 1943. The first arrivals took over administrative positions and a number of enlisted men were released for more essential duties.[30] Five of the women were assigned as instructors in the radio school.[31]

Members of the 797th WAC Company being sworn in as soldiers in the regular army. They became full-fledged GIs, committed to serving for the duration plus six months. *Center for Western Studies.*

Veterans of one year of service at the Sioux Falls ATS, these six WACs were the only ones remaining from the original cadre of fourteen sent to the Sioux Falls base on June 11, 1943. *Center for Western Studies.*

During the first week in July 1943, President Roosevelt signed an Act of Congress that made the Women's Auxiliary Army Corps a part of the regular army. The women would now have the same regulations which governed enlisted men and they were entitled to the same rights, benefits and privileges. The law became effective on September 1.[32] On August 30, the 797th WAAC Company was formally sworn in as members of the regular army. Henceforth, they were known as the Women's Army Corps (WAC). As members of the regular army, the women were obligated for the duration of the war plus six months.[33]

During the following months, most of the new WACs arriving at the base were assigned as radio operator instructors. They had been trained at the Midland Radio and Television School in Kansas City, Missouri. Their course consisted of 16 to 17 weeks in radio theory and 20 weeks of code instruction; 325 hours of code and 109 hours of hand sending were among the requirements for a Midland diploma.[34] At the ATS, black WACs were categorized as Squadron B-N. They served in various capacities, including nursing and as instructors.[35]

On the first anniversary of the WAC arrival at the ATS, only six remained of the original fourteen. But sixty-eight members of the Women's Army Corps were present and they received Good Conduct medals. They assumed many duties at the base, many of the jobs had been held by civilian women from the city. Several were assigned to the base headquarters. They served as clerks, stenographers, teletype operators and message center personnel. Others served in the post locator, the service club, motor pool, the station hospital, the general mess office and as instructors in the radio school.[36]

After the defeat of Japan, some of the military regulations for the WAC were relaxed. For example, they no longer were required to perform pre-dawn calisthenics. Swimming, roller skating, bowling, bicycling and horseback riding became more pleasurable substitutions.[37] During the mass demobilization that followed VJ Day, a point system was used to determine the order of discharge. The first women who were discharged from the WAC needed forty-four points.[38]

The war redefined the place of women in the workforce. They ably took over occupations that had been almost exclusively male prior to the war. The women became car and truck drivers, factory workers, engaged in field work on American farms and joined the thousands of "Rosie the Riveters" in producing America's weaponry. They took advantage of the economic opportunities as they displayed their patriotism.

With the demobilization of millions of men in 1945-1946, the majority of the women who had served so well were forced to resume their "traditional" roles as housewives, teachers, nurses and secretaries. But the women who had worked outside of the home were subtly and profoundly changed. They had gained a sense of independence and self-worth, and within two decades they began to experience economic and social gains.

Sioux Falls and the surrounding area did not experience some of the negatives associated with women in the workforce that took place in larger urban centers. Nationally, the number of women in the workforce reached 16.5 million, 36 percent of the labor force. During the war, the divorce rate increased substantially. With the absence of parental supervision, there were large numbers of "latch-key" children with the father being in the armed forces and the mother away at work. Juvenile delinquency increased as well as juvenile prostitution.

# Chapter 9

*You can't touch me, I'm in the Army.*
*– Benny the Bungler*

A cartoon that appeared in the *Polar Tech,* the base newspaper, depicted a soldier talking to a civilian policeman. Described as the famous last words of Benny the Bungler, the soldier said, "You can't touch me, I'm in the Army."[1] Although relations between the students at the Army Technical School and the Sioux Falls Police Department were generally good there were notable exceptions.

For a few months after the base opened, the city's court system had been lenient with the newly arrived soldiers. Several GIs had engaged in flagrant speeding, others were guilty of driving while intoxicated. Finally, Municipal Judge Walter Conway said enough was enough. He stated, "We felt that men in service deserved special consideration but now it seems that they are taking advantage of this generosity." Thus, he cracked down on traffic offenders. He began by fining ATS men $50 for driving while intoxicated.[2] Fines collected in May 1942 totaled $616. In June 1942, fines totaled $2,472. The number of arrests rose from 98 in May to 160 in June. Because of curtailed travel and a shortage of tires, the number of accidents actually declined from 66 to 49 in the same period.[3]

The Sioux Falls Police Department had been in disarray during the fall of 1942. The police chief, J. W. Galvin, made attempts to reform the force. He fired Walter Keith for not being on duty, the second such offense against him. William J. Miller was demoted from night patrol captain to patrolman until he wore a presentable uniform. Miller had also taken a vacation without official notice. After a hearing before the city commission, he was reinstated.[4]

On January 6, 1943, Galvin resigned to become the secretary for Mayor C. M. Whitfield. The mayor appointed Fred J. Searls to be the new police chief. Searls had been a former policeman and detective for the Sioux Falls Police Department for twelve years. Currently, he was serving as chief agent in charge of law enforcement for the South Dakota Attorney General's office.[5] Mayor Whitfield met with police department personnel on January 2 and called for an end to envy, back-biting and other glaring faults existing in the officers' ranks. He said that they had not given Galvin their full support. There had been too much criticism in public. In his closing statement, the mayor said, "The police department for a long period of time has never reached a satisfactory degree of operating efficiency. There is a lack of courtesy shown to the public. You have the impression that your position is secure because of civil service. In this you are mistaken."[6]

Fortunately, the city's police force had the support of the military police (MPs). The MPs located their headquarters in the police department, and from 1942-1945 there was close cooperation between the civilian and military authorities.[7] The police and the MPs had frequent calls to West 12th Street as bars and road houses lined the street as far west as the intersection of the Tea road and Highway 16. Located here was the infamous Yellow Lantern. Another notorious bar was the Riverview Inn, located south of Highway 16 on the banks of the Sioux River. The Cap D. Jones night club and tourist camp was declared off-limits to military personnel. Other places that had dance floors and juke boxes popular with soldiers were the Villa Milla, the Westward Ho, the Dynamite and King Richards. Some were not officially bars but places where a soldier carried his liquor bottles with him and prepared his own mixed drinks. Musicians from the base would often go to some of these places on weekends and provide live music for the revelers. The MPs would show up quite regularly and soldiers would be booked for public intoxication.[8] The editor of the *Argus Leader* echoed a survey taken by the Office of War Information (OWI) on drinking conditions around Army camps. After reviewing the results of the survey, OWI officials said, "There is no excessive drinking among troops and drinking does not constitute a serious problem." The editor of the local paper believed that conditions in Sioux Falls were excellent. In a benevolent mood, the editor felt the men at the ATS preferred to drink a rich, malted milk—the richer the better. Returning to the realm of reason, the editor concluded "that soldiers do drink but one rarely sees an intoxicated soldier in the streets."[9]

In the spring of 1943, two other sites were declared off limits. The female manager of the Northwestern Tavern was charged with illegal liquor sales. The Central Hotel on North Main Avenue was closed by the Fire and City Health departments, charged with seven counts of unsanitary conditions.

Sioux Falls police officers were kept busy not only with enforcement of the law among the civilian population but also with activities that impacted soldiers who were on liberty in the city. There was a continuous crackdown on bootleggers and on women from other communities charged with vagrancy or prostitution. Following fulfillment of their jail sentence, the women were told to leave the city.[10] The police would continue their strong efforts to make prostitutes understand that Sioux Falls did not welcome them.[11] The police blotter indicated that many GIs were fined $25 for speeding. ATS personnel were apprehended for tampering with downtown fire alarms. A few GIs were charged with auto theft and later abandoning the cars. Jewelry and currency were stolen at the Green Gables Cabin Camp on South Minnesota Avenue. On rare occasions, drunken ATS personnel were jailed for assaulting a policeman.[12] Illegal gambling, poker and slot machines were found in private homes usually followed by altercations if the GIs believed they were being cheated. There were several instances of soldiers engaging in check fraud, gaining money under false pretenses.[13] There were occasional acts of vandalism. For example, three young civilian males and two GIs picked up and smashed a manhole cover on a downtown street. The two soldiers were turned over to the military.[14]

The GIs often used taxi cabs to go from the base to downtown Sioux Falls. They were frequently victimized by unscrupulous cab drivers. The cabs were not equipped with meters and several of the cabbies continually overcharged the soldiers. The cab companies were unaware of what the drivers were doing. The editor of *Polar Tech* reminded the paper's readers that all cabs had the same rate—25 cents for the first two-thirds of a mile and five cents for each additional one-third of a mile. The writer urged GIs to read the speedometer when entering a cab. They were to check the reading again when they arrived at their destination and pay the correct amount.[15]

One cab driver experienced a costly lesson when he parked directly outside one of the air base gates waiting for a passenger. He learned that military jurisdiction extended 100 feet beyond the actual limits of the base and all entrances to the base were to be kept open for emergency operations. The cab was interfering with operations. MPs warned the unlucky and defiant driver three times to move but he refused to comply with the request. Colonel Cote arrived and ordered the cabbie to leave. The driver refused. Cote then ordered the MPs to shoot out a tire on the cab. They promptly flattened the left rear tire of the cab. The cabbie then drove a short distance away, changed the tire, and returned to the city with his passenger. Attorney M.T. Woods, representing Soo Cab, said the company would not take any action regarding the matter. The owner of Soo Cab said the officers at the Army base were doing a splendid job. He further stated, "So far as Soo Cab, Inc. are concerned they [the Army] are entitled to and will get our full cooperation."[16]

On occasion, a soldier would be absent without leave (AWOL) and the military police would be sent out to retrieve him after he had been located. There were some free spirits who would take a three-day pass whether they had received it or not. Often they would be found in a nearby community, such as Pipestone or Canton. The local police department would call the base and request that the MPs come and get their man.

On the front page of the *Polar Tech* would often appear a small box at the bottom of the right-hand column listing court-martial results for guilty men, many of them for being AWOL. They were usually sentenced to six months hard labor and forfeiture of pay for the same time period.[17]

One of the serious crimes at the base was stealing government property and delivering it to civilian co-conspirators in the city. Large cuts of meat disappeared from base freezers and precious copper wire from warehouses. At night, these valuable products made their way over the fence and into the waiting hands of "black marketeers." The thievery was discovered and the guilty GIs, following court-martial proceedings, were sent to the federal prison at Leavenworth, Kansas.[18]

Cases involving soldiers charged with misdemeanors and criminal activity were turned over to the Judge Advocate Department. The three officers assigned to the department were former attorneys. If charges against a soldier were not filed within twenty-four hours after his arrest, he usually returned to his squadron for duty. If charges were filed, and depending upon the seriousness of the offense, the soldier could be subjected to one of the three following types of court martial:

*Summary Court-Martial:* If the offense was minor, the man charged appeared before one officer appointed by the base's commanding officer. If the soldier was found guilty, the maximum sentence was reduction to private, confinement to hard labor for a month and the forfeiture of pay for one month.

*Special Court-Martial:* This court consisted of three or more officers appointed by the base commander. If found guilty by this court, the person charged with the offense was reduced to the grade of private, sentenced to hard labor for six months and the forfeiture of pay for six months.

*General Court-Martial:* Cases involving murder or desertion were handled by this court. The court was composed of five or more officers. If found guilty, the man was subject to dishonorable discharge, forfeiture of all pay and all allowances due to him and life imprisonment at hard labor or death.[19]

Several major crimes occurred in 1943. During the spring and early summer, several local women were assaulted by a private from the Army Technical School. The most serious attack occurred on May 11 when a twenty-year-old stenographer was assaulted while walking home after seeing a movie at the Granada Theater. She was dragged into an alley on Dakota Avenue between 9th and 10th streets. The woman was beaten severely but managed to make her way home unaided.[20] On May 30, a seventeen-year-old girl was chased by the soldier and thrown to the lawn in front of her own home. Her screams brought neighbors outdoors and the soldier fled.[21]

The incidents ended with the soldier's attack on a female air-raid warden during a blackout drill on June 21. The woman was thrown to the ground near 4th Street and Spring Avenue. Her screams brought two men to the scene who captured the soldier after chasing him for three blocks. The attacks were carried out by Private Manuel Soria. In a written statement, he admitted assaulting six different women in different areas of the city. With Soria's arrest, Police Chief Searls announced that the series of attack cases during recent months had been cleared up.[22]

The first of two murders occurred on January 25, 1943. The battered body of Mrs. Francis N. Orvedahl, age thirty-nine, the wife of a Lake Preston, South Dakota, physician, was found the following day in a Green Gables tourist cabin in South Sioux Falls. She had died from strangulation and brain injuries. The killer, Romeo E. Koethe, age thirty-eight, a native of Salem, South Dakota, was identified through transportation facilities and fingerprints taken at the cabin. Orvedahl and Koethe had registered at the tourist camp as Mr. and Mrs. Charles after a liquor party. She had applied for a position as an instructor at the air base. Keothe had formerly worked at the John Morrell meat-packing plant, Sioux Falls, and as an electrician at the ATS. Koethe, who had a criminal record, was arrested on a lesser charge in Rapid City on February 4, 1943.[23]

The most sensational and baffling murder case involving a person at the military base occurred on October 4, 1943. The victim was Second Lieutenant Naomi Kathleen Cheney, a member of the Women's Army Corps (WAC). A high school teacher from Jasper, Alabama, she graduated in 1942 from the Florida State College for Women, Tallahassee, Florida, with a degree in home economics. Cheney had taught one term of high school before joining the Women's Army Corps. The attractive woman with brown, curly hair had transferred to the Sioux Falls base eighteen days before her death.

On the night of her death, she asked the guard at the gate if it was safe for her to walk home alone. He told Cheney to use her own judgment. She left the base through Gate No. 3 on Northwest Street. After a meal of peas and ham at the Cataract Hotel, she continued her walk to her lodging on South Euclid Avenue, where she and her roommate had just moved.

Cheney's body was found the next afternoon by a ten-year-old girl looking for sumac leaves in a wooded area near 12th Street and Grange Avenue. Val Rae (Hill) Nedey said it was a beautiful, sunny afternoon when she encountered the lieutenant's body sprawled in the path. The child's parents notified the police. The body was in a small clearing in a weed-overgrown hollow about 100 feet south of the 12th Street bridge and fifty feet southwest of the railroad tracks.[24]

The city police and the military police conducted a thorough investigation of the crime scene and the adjacent area. An autopsy showed that Lieutenant Cheney died of a crushed skull due to a large blunt object or several kicks to the head. It was the only part of her body that had been touched. Her clothes were not torn and there was no evidence of rape. The coroner ruled it a homicide. Two days after the murder, the police brought in a suspect. A transient, living in a tourist cabin approximately fifty feet from where the lieutenant's body had been found, became the primary suspect. He was a farm laborer from Worthington, Minnesota, who had arrived in Sioux Falls a few days before the murder. He was known to have a wife and children in Iowa plus several girlfriends, one of whom worked at the air base.

The police found blood matching Cheney's type inside and outside the thirty-one-year-old transient's cabin. They were unable to make a better match using the technology available during the 1940s. According to retired police captain Mark Thorstenson, the transient got away with murder. The suspect was in close proximity, he had told certain falsehoods and there was the important factor of blood on his shoes and just outside his cabin door. The suspect said he had no idea how the blood had gotten there. As for the blood on his shoes, he said he had stepped outside the door in the morning into what he thought was jam. As Thorstenson argued, that did not explain the blood on the top of his shoes. The police captain theorized that the blood came from kicking Cheney in the head hard enough to fracture her skull.

One can only surmise possible motives for the killing. Among the possibilities suggested by Thorstenson was that Cheney and the killer knew one another through the transient's girlfriend at the base. They may have talked on her walk home. He may have convinced her to come to his cabin. He may have made sexual advances and violence ensued. At about 9:30 P.M., a woman, about two blocks south, had heard a scream and rustling noises. The transient was seen stumbling out of the cabin to vomit.

With inconclusive evidence, the suspect was released. He was due to be inducted into the Army. Records indicate that he died overseas during World War II. Retired detective Herman Ostlund felt that the military impeded the investigation, that the local police were thwarted by the military police. He believed the MPs were more interested in winning the war than the murder of one of their personnel. There is no question that if the suspect's shoes and Cheney's blood were available, modern technology would provide a match leading to an indictment. The crime remains unsolved to this day.

Cheney's murder stunned the community. Some citizens, who were already suspicious of the large military presence, became leery of soldiers. Overall, relations between base personnel and the civilian population continued to be positive. It is remarkable that more crimes were not committed, given the huge, diverse body of men located adjacent to the city of Sioux Falls.

# Chapter 10

*After seeing some of the crowded buses that travel between the Base and the city, we would not be surprised if the bus company used the slogan "The public be jammed."*
*– Polar Tech, July 27, 1944*

After a day of study in the classroom analyzing circuits, studying the tech order system and learning tuning procedure, maintenance and transmission, students looked forward to engaging in some of the activities available on the base for relief from the stress acquired in the school room.  Given the number of activities available, there was little reason for boredom.  Although the students lived in a regulated society for four to five months, there were many amenities available at this military base, which had emerged so dramatically near the Big Sioux River.  Life was much more than barracks and school buildings.

## MEETING MATERIAL NEEDS

The Army Air Base, where the technical school was located, had no main street but there were eight stores, two filling stations, a post exchange, a laundry, landing field and dental and hospital facilities.  There were three chapels (and nine chaplains), two movie theaters and a sports arena.  The filling stations resembled frontier claim shacks except for the gasoline pumps out front.  The stores included a photo finishing service, a shoe repair shop, barber and tailor shops (including two female barbers) and the post exchange or general store, where one could purchase candy and tobacco, fountain drinks, jewelry and clothing.[1]  The post exchange was a very busy place during the Christmas holidays.  Toys, jewelry, luggage, drug and sundry items plus a full line of winter clothing were among the frequent purchases.  Jewelry for loved ones back home was a favorite item.  Famous brands of wristwatches were priced from $10 to $50.

Brooches could be purchased for $2.50, sterling earrings for $3.75, beads for $10, diamond pendants for $10, and music boxes for $6. A parcel wrapping center was available, too, for those men who would rather not make the attempt.[2]

Laundry facilities on the base were limited until 1943. For a while, the downtown laundries were kept busy.[3] Two months after the first contingent of men began classes at the Army Technical School, a contract was awarded to the Sioux Syndicate Company for between $100,000 and $500,000 for the construction of a temporary frame building and a steam plant.[4] This facility was not capable of supplying the laundry needs of 28,000 to 30,000 men. As a result, students were charged a transportation fee of ninety cents per week because most

This is not a South Dakota claim shack! It is one of the service stations at the Army Air Base. *Center for Western Studies.*

of the laundry was sent to cities as much as 225 miles away. Most of the laundry was sent to Minneapolis and St. Paul laundries.

In late February 1943, a new quartermaster laundry opened at the base. It was located near Covell Lake, now the current site of the Veterans' Memorial Park.[5] Each student was charged $1.50 per month to use its services. No limit was set on the number of articles that could be sent in one large bundle, but only one bundle per week could be sent. The charge was made whether the soldier sent his laundry or not unless excused by the commanding officer, sick in the hospital, on furlough, detached service awaiting shipment or AWOL. No soldier was to combine his laundry with someone else's. If a GI sent his laundry during the last two weeks of the month, he would pay a minimum rate of fifty cents for a bundle of thirty pieces.

Huge machines put soiled laundry through soap, seven changes of temperature and forty-five minutes of steady washing. There was a flat-work iron for sheets. Facilities for dry cleaning clothes were available at the post exchange.

## CHOW HOUNDS AT PARK PLAZA

Under normal circumstances, active young men have large appetites and the Army realized that food was very important for GI morale. The students at the ATS received more than 3,000 calories a day. Army dietitians stressed that meals should consist of 10 percent protein, 60 percent carbohydrates and 30 percent fats. The mess officer used a worldwide master menu provided by the Quartermaster General and the Surgeon General's office. Perishable foods were purchased through the Quartermaster Marketing Center in Kansas City. Dry foods were purchased directly from the producers or manufacturers. Vitamin C held the lead among vitamins. Stress was placed on citrus fruits and leafy green and yellow vegetables.

From 1942 to the spring of 1945 there were only two large mess halls. Crowded conditions caused by the influx of personnel being redeployed or separated from the service necessitated the opening of three additional mess halls in 1945. Workers in the mess halls were kept busy sixteen to twenty-four hours per day cleaning vegetables.[6] The General Mess Office followed a strict ration plan. The monthly allowance of ration points for a soldier was equal in some cases to twice the amount allotted to civilians.[7]

Soldiers standing in line awaiting entrance into the Park Plaza, Ritz Carlton, or just plain "Mess Hall." *Center for Western Studies*.

As the war progressed, more quick fresh frozen fruit and vegetables were used, since obtaining canned goods was difficult. When fluid milk also became more difficult to secure, ice cream was served four times a week. Roasts and steaks were dear to the "chow hounds." Meat was a major part of the state-side soldier's diet. Other kinds of meat were used in different ways. Other popular items on the menu were fish, cheese, eggs, poultry, whole-grain bread and cereal.[8]

The average cost for feeding soldiers was about fifty-six cents each day. The average at the Sioux Falls base was about four cents higher than the national average due to the higher cost of fresh vegetables. In the fall of 1942, radiomen consumed approximately six pounds of beef, over ten quarts of milk, two pounds of butter, a pound of coffee and two pounds of sugar each month.[9]

Mess hall workers served twenty-five men per minute as they streamed in from well coordinated lines by groups and squadrons. Men in the first shift got up at 5 A.M. and raced to the mess halls by the light of the moon.[10] The mess halls were of frame construction and sported several no-smoking signs on the interior walls. There was no idle conversation as the men ate their meals, and they did not linger after finishing. If one shift took longer than necessary for a meal, the subsequent group became agitated. If a group did loiter at meal time, the following group had its chance for revenge later.

Mess hall workers were Army-trained cooks and bakers fresh from technical schools, as were the men who served on the food line. The base bakery was located in one of the mess halls. A staff sergeant and twenty-three enlisted men made up the work force in the bakery.[11]

Occasionally, students did handle some of the food, such as removing eyes from the potatoes. As was customary in the military service, the GIs groused about the food while thriving on it. Large numbers of men added pounds while in training.

Every morning, personnel went to the ice house in Sioux Falls, where they checked and loaded large chunks of ice to be used in the mess halls throughout the day. Two shifts of permanent workers were attached to each mess hall to speed food preparation, further enhanced by modern equipment. An automatic potato peeler cleaned a sack of potatoes, except for the eyes, in ten minutes. The kitchens had batteries of electric mixers, slicing machines, cooking utensils and water softening machines. A customary Sunday dinner included chicken, French baked potatoes and tasty lemon pie.[12] On March 1, 1943, in an attempt to relieve the burden placed upon food producing facilities and to reduce waste, the daily ration allowance was to be based on the actual number of men fed at mess daily. It was a departure from the old practice that based rations on the number of men shown in squadron morning reports. All men were urged to eat in the mess halls as it would make for a more accurate estimate of the food required. The men were assured that their diet would be adequate and there would be no change in the quality of food. The mess halls had been allotted funds from which to purchase their requirements. Supplies would come from the quartermaster.[13]

Journalists who were given permission to visit the base were usually taken to lunch at one of the mess halls. They sat together at long tables and ate what the soldiers ate. According to the journalists, the food, served cafeteria style, was excellent. Marie Christopherson, a columnist for the *Argus Leader*, wrote that the menu for the day included rich, yellow cheese, assorted cold meats, a large portion of potato salad with onions and greens, sweet pickles, white bread, whole milk and pear sauce that tasted homemade.[14]

If some of the GIs had complaints regarding weekday meals, no one could complain about the Christmas Day menu. It certainly contributed to the celebratory mood. The menu included the following: vegetable soup, saltines, roast milk-fed turkey, sage dressing, snowflake potatoes, giblet gravy, creamed corn, lettuce with Russian dressing, cranberry sauce, mince pies, ice cream, chocolate nut cake, assorted fresh fruit, candies and nuts, coffee, evaporated milk, sugar, bread and butter.[15]

Although the food was certainly adequate at the base, the GIs looked forward to eating at restaurants in the city. When the Technical School went on a six-day week in the spring of 1944, more men had Sunday off, placing a burden on Sioux Falls restaurants. During these years, restaurants were contending with food rationing and an acute shortage of help. The editor of *Polar Tech* urged the men to eat their Sunday dinner in the base mess halls as they served their best meals at this time.[16]

During April 1943, seventy-nine officers, enlisted men and civilian employees, requested garden plots. Like their counterparts in Sioux Falls, they wanted to have "Victory Gardens." The administration honored their request and each person who made a request was assigned a 25' x 50' garden plot. The procurement of seed, garden tools, and upkeep was the responsibility of the grower. The resulting produce belonged to the grower. The enlisted men's gardens were located just south of the laundry. The officers' gardens were across from the Bachelor Officers Quarters (BOQ). Civilian plots were located outside of the base fence south of Gate 2.[17]

During the spring of 1944, the number of personnel interested in having "Victory Gardens" doubled with plots similar in size to those of the preceding year. Growers were free to use the produce as they wished. The enlisted men chose to have their harvest of vegetables used in the squadron and detachment mess halls.[18]

Soldiers who were married and lived off-base with their families had their own source of foodstuffs. A complete grocery store was established on the base. The commissary sales store, run by the Quartermaster Corps, was located in Warehouse 18.[19] Food was stocked on shelves in alphabetical order corresponding to the inventory listing, facilitating shopping and frequent taking of inventory.[20]

Displayed on the shelves were fresh vegetables, choice steaks and canned goods. Two civilian butchers were present to prepare the meat for sale. The foodstuffs were shipped by rail from the Chicago Quartermaster Depot. Regulations dictated that all food arriving at the base had to be unloaded within twenty-four hours after arrival. Prices at the commissary were considerably lower than those in civilian stores. The Chicago Quartermaster Depot provided the price list for most commodities. The majority of the customers were soldiers' wives. They did not worry about prices. They were more concerned about ration points. For each ounce of specified food, ration points were needed. Their husbands applied for ration stamps at the local OPA office. The wives of the GIs had to present their ration books each time they went to Warehouse 18. They often spoke of "ration point blues."[21]

## TRANSPORTATION AND COMMUNICATION

There were four railroad companies providing service for Sioux Falls in 1942: the Great Northern, the Illinois Central, the Milwaukee Road and the Rock Island. The Milwaukee Road was the leading carrier of troops to and from Sioux Falls when soldiers departed for new assignments elsewhere. Their lady loves always saw them off. One wit said it was a good spot to pick up some pointers on techniques.[22]

To speed up the handling of freight at the base, two-and-one-half miles of track were laid, connecting the commercial rail lines and warehouses at the end of the base. There were six spur tracks linked to the main track. The base had its own locomotive, a twenty-ton gasoline powered engine. Five soldiers who had civilian railroading experience served as the train crew. The locomotive could move heavily loaded freight cars with ease. It was used to pull as many as nine cars.[23]

The editor of *Polar Tech* stated that 8th and Phillips in Sioux Falls was a plot of ground entirely surrounded by taxi cabs containing eleven people including the driver. The cry was heard, "Go ahead and get in, there's always room for one more." Taxis were much in demand but buses played a major role in transporting personnel within the confines of the base and to and from the city. In one year, 1943, the number of bus employees increased from thirty-five to eighty-one to meet the demand. The growth of bus service was attributed to the increase in traffic and gas rationing. The buses within the base operated from 5:00 A.M to 2:30 A.M. the following day. The officer of the day helped to keep things moving, preventing any tie-ups.[24]

Base personnel published an excellent newspaper with some of its stories republished in the city's daily newspaper. The first edition of *Polar Tech*, at forty-eight pages, came off the press on August 16, 1942. It was distributed to all subscribers of the *Argus Leader* but delivered to personnel at the base on Friday, August 21, only after the deletion of a story ordered by Colonel Cote. The paper went on to achieve national recognition. In May 1944, the University of Missouri School of Journalism selected *Polar Tech* as the Number One GI publication in the nation based on its February 1944 issue. For three consecutive years, *Polar Tech* rated among the best service publications in the world according to Camp Newspaper Services' annual judging contest. Staff Sergeant Jack Fleischer became the editor of the paper in May 1943.

The last issue of *Polar Tech* came out in mid-June 1945. It occurred as the Technical School ceased operations and the administration of the base was assumed by the 2nd Air Force. The paper was renamed the *Sioux Sentinel*.[25] As the draw down of military personnel was reaching its final phase, the last issue of the *Sioux Sentinel* was published on November 30, 1945.

A broadcasting system for the base became effective on September 30, 1943. In its early stages, the system reached all areas of the ATS with the exception of the mess halls. They became a part of the system when loudspeakers arrived. The 1300-watt system was designed by Sergeant Edward M. Scribner, Schoharie, New York, with the help of two assistants. Scribner was a self-taught engineer who designed and installed radio equipment.[26] There were long delays in getting materials but the complete system went into operation on October 20, 1943. At first, thirty-six large speakers were placed in squadron streets with other speakers added later.

The system eventually brought a full daily schedule of programs to the radio school. Personnel received recorded bugle calls, announcements, marching music, popular music, important news via the Associated Press wire (teletype machine). They installed a direct NBC wire to feed in many of the network's top broadcasts. There was a direct wire to local radio stations KSOO and KELO. Scribner and colleagues created a soundproof studio large enough to accommodate an orchestra and other entertainers. The broadcast facilities included studios, offices and a control room. They were located in the left wing of Building 13 near base headquarters. Scribner was the broadcast engineer.[27] He was chosen as soldier of the week for his accomplishments.[28]

## ENTERTAINMENT

Music was the favorite form of entertainment at the Army Technical School. Wherever there was a piano, whether at the Service Club or in one of the day rooms located in the barracks, someone would be playing the piano with a group of students gathered around singing songs from memory or sheet music. If instruments were available, talented GIs would gather with the pianist and enjoy playing jazz or riffs on various songs.

There was an abundance of musical talent among the Permanent Party and the students. An Army Air Forces band was formed in July 1942 beginning with a nucleus of four musicians. A year later it was composed of thirty-two members, a large number having had professional experience.[29] In its first year, the band performed at more than a hundred events, including military events, community parades, and marching down Phillips Avenue. They wore helmet liners and leggings during the parades, bond drives and at daily retreat. They were part of a huge human cross on Easter morning.[30] The band played at troop inspections and reviews when a visiting general was at the base. On Memorial Day, June 1944, following an address by Governor M.Q. Sharpe, they accompanied a review of the troops by Sharpe and Colonel Oscar Rogers.[31] A base orchestra, the Didahdiers, was called on frequently to play for squadron dances. Thanks to the aforementioned Mrs. Goodrich, there were always plenty of charming Techettes, Military Misses and Khaki Pals available for partners. The young women were provided by local organizations. Men were also

A local woman leads a sing-along at the Army Technical School. *Center for Western Studies.*

permitted to bring their own dates.[32] Many of the dances were held in the base gymnasium and went on from 8:30 P.M. until midnight, concluding with the orchestra playing "Good Night Ladies." In 1942, 200 girls were issued permanent invitations for dances by being given small cardboard tags that had to be worn to gain admittance to the base.[33]

A formal Glee Club was established and it performed at community functions and the annual graduation ceremonies that were often held at either a base theater or the Sioux Falls Coliseum. Instrumental and choral groups performed for organizations and churches in Sioux Falls.

Whenever a nationally known organization stopped in Sioux Falls to perform at the Arkota Ballroom, on their way from Chicago to cities on the West Coast, they usually played a free concert for the servicemen. One of the first of the "Big Bands" to arrive was the Louis Armstrong Orchestra in September 1942. "Satchmo" returned for another concert in May 1944. Other big bands that played before

ATS personnel were those of Jack Teagarden, Kay Keyser, Jan Savett, Bobby Sherwood and Charlie Spivak. More than 10,000 soldiers and civilians gathered to listen to an outdoor concert by the Tommy Dorsey Orchestra playing swing and sweet music. In August 1944, the Duke Ellington Orchestra, which had an engagement at the Arkota, played two performances at one of the base theaters. Nearly 3,000 GIs packed the theater and hundreds of men were turned away before the scheduled start of the concerts.

Personnel at the ATS were also entertained by visiting USO Camp Shows that emphasized songs and a variety of vaudeville acts. An occasional celebrity showed up at the base. Tech Sergeant Gene Autry, a Western movie star, who had joined the army in April 1942, presented a show at the base in May 1943. Because his horse, Champion, was not present, Autry chose one of the horses used by sentinels when they patrolled the perimeter of the base during the night.[34] Jesse Owens, an American hero in the 1936 summer Olympics staged a race with two stalwart black soldiers (see Chapter 7).

Each year, base personnel in conjunction with the Sioux Falls community scheduled a musical at the Sioux Falls Coliseum. The "GI Follies" presented *Sky High* in October 1943. The proceeds from these performances were directed to financing the construction of a swimming pool (see Chapter 6), which was to be used by base personnel and then turned over to the city at the end of World War II.[35] One of the most popular base-community musicals was the production of Rogers and Hammerstein's *Oklahoma!* In October 1944, students from the base staged Maxwell Anderson's prize-winning play *The Eve of St. Mark*. It was staged using original music scores and unique scenery and lighting.[36]

If students had leisure time, primarily on Sunday, they could always go to the day room or to the service club. The day rooms, located in certain barracks had nothing aesthetic or fancy about them. But it was a place to relax and many contained radios, pool and ping-pong tables, a Coke machine, a pay phone, writing desks and a few magazines. A few day rooms were fortunate enough to have out-of-tune pianos.

The ATS service club provided additional amenities. There was a cafeteria with a soda fountain on one side of the building. The club contained a quiet and spacious reading room. There was a library that early in 1944 contained 9,000 volumes plus eighteen magazines

A day room at the Army Technical School, where students could relax. *Center for Western Studies.*

and newspapers from twenty-eight cities.[37] There was a music library. Lovers of the classics could listen to music ranging from the operettas of Victor Herbert to Tchaikovsky's *Fifth Symphony*.[38] GIs could use the city library by purchasing a $1.00 card. The dollar was returned when the soldier was transferred to another base. The city librarian said that the students made significant use of the library. There were occasions when a GI needed additional money. He would go to the library and tell the librarian that he was being transferred which was untrue. Perhaps a week later, he would return with a dollar, usually after a pay day and secure another card.

In the lounge one could find a quiet corner to write a letter to one's family or to a "special someone" back home. A man was available to record a message that a GI could send home free of charge.[39] The club also had a recreation room where games were available, such as chess, checkers, table tennis, and jigsaw puzzles.[40] With the base's abundance of talent, the piano was in constant use with the pianist playing boogie-woogie, sweet music and the popular songs of the day. On Sundays, there was some informal dancing. Dances at the club were usually held twice a week and a formal dance once a month. Programs were arranged three times a week by two fulltime hostesses. Usually, they were Red Cross assistants who worked without pay.[41]

The service club lounge was the most popular meeting place for sons and daughters to gather with their visiting families. The base played host to more than 200 mothers on Mother's Day in May 1943. They came from all parts of the nation to spend the day with their sons and daughters. They were met at the train and bus depots and transported to the base in Army vehicles. They were housed for the night in the WAAC barracks and ate in the mess halls with their sons and daughters on Sunday. The mothers attended a special Mother's Day service in one of the chapels, followed by an extensive tour of the base, and participated in a "Sundown Dance."

Special activities were arranged for Christmas and Easter. During the year-end holiday period, a Christmas decoration contest was staged with prizes given to the best decorated exteriors of barracks.[42] As discussed earlier, on Easter morning, thousands of people from Sioux Falls and the surrounding area attended a sunrise service at the base at which time the troops formed a large cross.[43] The base also had clubs for officers and non-commissioned officers (NCOs). It featured dining facilities, a large dance floor, game rooms

Non-commissioned officers check their mail. *Courtesy Doug Uthe.*

that contained billiard tables, and other amenities similar to those in the service club.[44]

## CHOOSE YOUR GAME

The students at the Army Technical School could choose to participate in a variety of indoor and outdoor sports. For many of the men, there were more athletic facilities available on the base than in the communities from which they had recently departed. Supervised athletic programs, including basketball, boxing, judo wrestling and bowling, were among the sports in which GIs could choose to participate.[45] There were intra-squadron ball games and base championships, but for many men and women these activities were just a form of exercise. A modern track was constructed near the Arena and there was a roller rink with free skating for military personnel.[46] Later, a larger new rink that was covered by a tent with open sides was constructed. The open sides ensured skaters a maximum of summer comfort. During the winter, an ice rink was created and named Sodako.

Baseball was played at Howard Wood Field with two base teams, the Marauders and the Raiders, participating in league play. A softball field was located on the base as well as a makeshift football field. A tennis court was available and a golf course was created on the south side of the hospital zone.[47] Twenty sets of golf clubs and twenty dozen balls were available without charge to military personnel. The fairways were grass-seeded and the hard surface greens were composed of oil treated with sand. There were regular sand traps and bunkers near the greens. As related earlier, the construction of a swimming pool near Covell Lake was completed in mid-summer 1944. The Special Service Division placed a number of small boats on Covell Lake with enlisted men to supervise activity at all times. A limit of one hour was placed on each ride, but if there were GIs waiting in line, rides were limited to a half hour.[48] During the winter months, skis were available through the USO for those soldiers who wished to ski down the hill in Sherman Park.[49]

Usually, once a week, weather permitting, the men were ordered to the obstacle course. It gave the men the opportunity to "work off steam" and improve their physical condition. Part of the course gained the title "the birth of the bruise," a pun on a popular song of

Soldiers and their girls proceed cautiously at the base roller rink. *Center for Western Studies.*

the time. One obstacle that was no friend to the majority of the men was an eight-foot-high climbing wall. There were also the usual drill exercises and forced marches that all ex-GIs still remember.

## HEALTHCARE

On-the-job injuries, contagious diseases and pneumonia were among the most significant causes for hospitalization at the base. If not too ill and in the convalescent stage, students were placed in a program to combat boredom and mental fatigue. The objective of the program was to maintain or rekindle their interest in military matters and normal base duties through programs of physical drill and educational instruction. The recreational and reconditioning program, including some rehabilitation work and orthopedic training, achieved remarkable results in keeping students apace of their classes while convalescing. It saved hours of instruction they would not have taken when released from the hospital. They were kept abreast of code sending and receiving in an adjacent building where keys and receivers were available.[50]

Patients received ten to thirty minutes a day of exercise depending on their condition. For one day each week, lectures and technical films on first aid, chemical warfare, current events, airplane identification and military courtesy were offered. Records of attendance were kept and when discharged from the hospital, certificates of completion were given.

A new dental clinic opened on the base on June 1, 1943. It contained twelve chairs plus a large room where dental records were kept and a well-equipped laboratory for making dentures, inlays and bridges.[51] The emphasis was on preventive dentistry. There were four categories for treating patients. Category four indicated that the patient's teeth were in good shape. People in category one presented teeth that needed immediate attention (extraction or trench mouth). A category two indicated a GI needed fillings and a number three person needed false teeth. The dentists averaged 200 sittings a day.[52]

In mid-May 1943, the federal government announced that Sioux Falls would be granted a veterans' hospital. The initial plan called for building on available land at the site of the Army Technical School. The hospital zone would be detached from all base buildings.[53] A month later, attention shifted to Columbus College, Sioux Falls, as a favored site. The Catholic Church Chancery had offered to sell the site plus forty adjoining acres to the government. Options had been secured to sell the site. At the time it was the location of St. Bernard Seminary. After it was determined to be unwise to build at the ATS, General Frank T. Hines, administrative director of the Veterans' Administration approved the establishment of the Royal C. Johnson Veterans Hospital at the site of the former Columbus College.[54]

## ORDER AND SECURITY

Discipline and a certain amount of regimentation were found at every military base in the United States, including the Sioux Falls Army Technical School. Daily inspection of the barracks was a part of military life. The enlisted men at the ATS had a new name for the officers who made daily inspections. They called them the "Gigstapo."[55] If a soldier's bunk or clothing was in disorder, he received a "gig" and an accumulation of gigs led to the loss of base privileges for a period of time.[56] The staff sergeant and lieutenant who daily inspected the barracks of Squadron 803 were accompanied by "Sergeant Buck." Buck was a dog who had the ability to find dirty undershirts and socks.[57]

Military police who patrolled base streets had the use of "First Sarge," a jeep driven by an enlisted man accompanied by a lieutenant. On their patrols they corrected and surprised soldiers who walked around with their hands in their pockets, who had unbuttoned coats or were walking two abreast. Attached to the jeep was a loudspeaker used by the officers to address the guilty, ordering them to adhere to base regulations. On the sides of the jeep were depicted a first sergeant's stripes, a purple heart and a Good Conduct insignia. According to military police lore, the jeep had earned a purple heart because of a burnt-out clutch and a Good Conduct emblem because every first sergeant should wear one of them.[58]

The dog "Sergeant Buck" assists early morning barracks inspectors. Buck was an expert at pointing out dirty clothes under a bunk. *Center for Western Studies*.

The jeep known as "First Sarge" roamed the base streets with a driver and officer and, using a loudspeaker, warned surprised GIs who walked around with their hands in their pockets or whose coats were unbuttoned. *Center for Western Studies.*

The base MPs had a staff car and two reconnaissance vehicles equipped with radio sets and men who mounted foot patrol between 1915 (7:15 P.M.) and 0500 (5:00 A.M.) had "handy talkie" portable sending and receiving sets to keep in contact with base headquarters. The battery operated set had a range of 1.5 miles with battery power for fourteen hours.

Among the many rules at the ATS was the recommendation for disposal of cigarettes. The regulation stated, "When through with a cigarette you are to crumble the butt between your thumb and index finger. You are to drop the remaining tobacco on the ground. Then you are to roll the cigarette paper into a minute ball and toss that away separately. If a breeze catches the paper before you have finished with the rolling process and carried it away, it is part of your duty to pick up those papers."[59] One could argue that this part of Army discipline was a waste of time. The war could not be won by picking up cigarette butts. Drill and studies were more important.

Throughout the war, the Sioux Falls Army Technical School had one of the lowest AWOL rates of any major installation in the Central Training Command.[60] The AWOL record for December 1943 was a little more than one-fortieth of one percent.[61] Much earlier, Colonel Cote ordered the *Polar Tech* staff to put a box at the bottom of column one, page one, indicating the decisions of court-martial trials. Guilty men were sentenced to six months of hard labor and forfeiture of pay for the same period of time.[62] For the last quarter of 1943, the number of General and Special Courts-Martial was lower than that of any other major station in the command. The base Judge Advocate presided at court-martial proceedings. Lieutenant J. E. Shannon was one of the special court officers. This was the same J. E. Shannon who assumed command of the 803rd African-American Squadron after its arrival at the base.

The Judge Advocate had a mock tombstone made by the base engineers. One was placed on the bunk of any man charged with being absent without leave. The tombstone, twenty-six inches tall and sixteen inches wide, remained on the absentee's bunk until his return. The pseudo-tombstone contained the GI's name and the number of days he was AWOL. The Judge Advocate commented that the man's AWOL "left us his work to do as well as our own."[63]

One of the best stories, perhaps apocryphal, to come out of the ATS involved a corporal who had been married a few days before coming to one of the nine base chaplains seeking a three-day pass for a honeymoon. He approached the chaplain with a Bible in hand and with one of his fingers on the following passage from Deuteronomy 24:5: "When a man is newly wed, he shall not go out with the army or be charged with any business; he shall be free at home one year to

This collage represents the judicial process at the Army Technical School: (clockwise) the offender is identified by his fingerprints, interviewed by the Judge Advocate's Office, and then faces court-martial. Lt. J.E. Shannon is shown at the extreme left, and in the center insert is Major C.T. Flota, Judge Advocate for the school. *Center for Western Studies.*

be happy with his wife whom he has taken." His plea for a three-day pass was denied.

## THE PASS SYSTEM

There was considerable experimentation with the Pass System at the Army Technical School, but there were two systems that had the greater longevity. There was a system for guests and one for the students based on their performance in the classroom. The first system was introduced in February 1943 and concerned female guests, a family member or dear friend desiring to visit with a GI. The guest was not permitted to register at a local hotel until certain requirements were met. The student, hoping to meet with an out-of-town guest, had to submit a letter to the Provost Marshal at least twenty-four hours in advance stating the name, home address and his relationship with the particular female. The letter also had to be approved by the soldier's squadron commander. When arriving in the city, the prospective guest first had to go to Military Police headquarters in the Sioux Falls City Hall where she was given an ID card. The woman presented the ID card when registering at the hotel. Proceeding to the base, the guest reported to the Provost Marshal's office at Gate 2. After presenting the ID card, the guest was escorted to the service club where she met with the waiting GI. The city police were the primary motivators for the foregoing procedure. They scanned hotel registrations as part of the program to prevent prostitutes from establishing their trade in the city.[64]

Every soldier also had to carry a pass when leaving the base. Their grades determined the length of time of the pass. Students whose grades were 85 and above received a green pass that granted special privileges. Students achieving grades of 70 to 84 received a blue weekend pass. A yellow pass was really no pass. It restricted a student to the base until he raised his grade to 70 or above in the next phase of his studies.[65] In mid-March 1943, photo IDs replaced the old pass cards but the student's academic status continued to be determined using the old grade system.[66]

Curfew restrictions applied to all passes. Soldiers were required to be off the streets and out of all public places by midnight except on Saturdays when the time was extended to 2:00 A.M. As the war with Japan was drawing to a close, a new curfew was set on July 20, 1945, with a uniform deadline of 1:30 A.M. for every day of the week.[67]

## FIRE DEPARTMENT

There were three fire stations at the base. Each station had a full staff of trained firefighters. All of the forty-eight firemen were civilians and, except for the fire chief, were eligible for the draft, causing a loss of personnel from time to time. The first fire chief was W. L. Perryman, a former employee of the Sioux Falls Fire Department. He attained the rank of captain before his retirement from the local force. His successor at the base was Louis M. Eitreim. The Central Fire Station at the base was in the warehouse area. The other two stations were located at Elkhorn Street and Second Avenue and Algonquin Street and Arapahoe Avenue. They had five pieces of rolling equipment: two 750 gallons per minute, two 500 gallon pumpers and a crash truck which operated at the flying field. There were no major fires until the collision of the two A-18s in December 1944. There was an earlier fire in the bitter January cold in Barracks 1429. The firemen put it out in less than four minutes.[68]

# Chapter 11

*Roses are red, Violets are Blue, Sugar is
sweet, Remember?
– Walter Winchell, radio and
newspaper commentator*

Away from the sea of khaki on Phillips and Main Avenues, the citizens of Sioux Falls adjusted their lifestyle to the needs and problems created by the war. There would be shortages and government controls. Travel by automobile would be limited by gasoline allotments and the lack of available new tires. In addition, there was mental stress within families if they had a son in "harm's way" overseas. War threatened the tranquility of their lives but it also promised economic opportunity. With the presence of the Army Technical School, people began to believe that the city had a greater economic destiny than merely continuing as an agricultural service center where farmers sold their grain and livestock.

## RATIONING

Shortly after the United States entered World War II, most grocery and meat prices still reflected Great Depression prices. A grocery ad in the June 25, 1942, *Argus Leader* listed the following prices for foods consumed in many Sioux Falls homes:

| | | | |
|---|---|---|---|
| Eggs | 28 cents per dozen | Flour | 89 cents for a 24.5 lb. bag |
| Potatoes | 35 cents for a 10 lb. bag | Bread | 2 cents for 1.5 lb. loaf |
| Sugar | 6.5 cents per pound | Bacon | 17 cents for a half lb. |
| Ham | 33 cents a pound | Butter | 35 cents per lb. |

| Carrots | 2 bunches for 15 cents | Beef Roast | 26 cents per lb. |
| Milk | 12 cents per quart | Bananas | 1.5 lbs. for 12 cents[1] |
| Coffee | 2 lbs. for 59 cents | | |

With more money exchanging hands, personal income in South Dakota increased from $360 in 1940 to $1,497 in 1948.[2] Sioux Falls housewives went grocery shopping at Red Owl, Sunshine, O.P. Skaggs, and the Economy Center Markets or at one of the many smaller grocery stores in the city.[3] Shopping for groceries, however, soon became more complicated as fighting in North Africa, Europe and in the Pacific Ocean intensified. The Office of Price Administration was established (OPA). Its mission was to prevent spiraling prices, the rising cost of living, profiteering, and inflation. The Emergency Price Control Act of January 30, 1942, gave the OPA significant powers. The General Maximum Price Regulation Act of April 28, 1942, affected about 60 percent of all civilian food items. Prices that were frozen at March 1, 1942, levels also applied to rental properties. On May 9, 1943, ceiling prices were set on other foodstuffs. Eight days later, on May 17, the OPA set ceiling prices on meat. As an illustration, T-bone steak sold for 59 cents a pound. As the war drew on, nearly every item Americans ate, wore, used, or lived in was rationed or otherwise regulated. The OPA's objectives to keep inflation down and to ensure the fair distribution of consumer goods proved very effective as prices on food rose only nine percent from 1942 to 1945.[4]

Rationing became a way of life. Prior to the war, people were familiar only with postal stamps. On a balmy night in early May 1942, local families began their monthly walk to local schools where teachers and volunteers issued the war ration books, one book for each member of a family. One Sioux Falls housewife was on her way to the hospital for the delivery of her second child. She stopped at Lowell Elementary School to get ration books. She wanted to have them when her family needed them. When asked how many people were in her family, she replied, "By tonight there will be four of us." She was allotted stamps for four people. The federal government provided families with ration books containing red, blue, brown and green stamps. There were blue stamps for purchasing canned goods, fruits and vegetables and red stamps for meat and dairy products. There were forty-eight coupons (or stamps) per person, per month, in the blue books. There were sixty-four coupons per person, per month, in the red books. When grocery shopping, housewives were more concerned with making their allotment of coupons last a month than the cost of their purchases. Clerks in grocery stores and meat markets were ordered not to accept single coupons torn from a book. They were to be removed from the families' ration books by the clerk or removed by the purchaser in his sight. Each person was allowed two pounds of meat each week.[5] Many adhered to the government's plea for "meatless Tuesdays." The number of coupons needed for a particular item was posted in the store. The following are the coupons required for several items:

| 1 lb. of hamburger | 7 coupons |
| 1 lb. of ham | 7 coupons |
| 1 lb. of butter | 16 coupons |
| 1 16 oz. can of peaches | 18 coupons |
| 48 oz. can of pineapple | 22 coupons |
| 1 lb. of porterhouse steak | 12 coupons[6] |

Sugar was the first table item to be rationed. Grocers were ordered to sell only ten-pound packages. The regulation of sugar purchases continued to 1946. Unfortunately, a certain amount of hoarding and bootlegging of sugar took place. Canned goods were added to the rationed list because tin was needed to pack rations for the military. Coffee was rationed in November 1942. German submarine activity along the Atlantic seaboard resulted in many American merchant ships being sunk bringing products from Latin America. Other commodities in short supply were coconut, pineapple, bananas, chocolate chips and, interestingly enough, Jell-O. In February 1943, there were only three boxes of lime Jell-O on the shelf in one of the city's largest grocery stores.[7]

Shoe rationing was put into effect in February 1943. Each person would be allowed three pairs of shoes. By 1944, however, only two pairs of shoes could be purchased. Shoes were rationed because fifteen million pairs of combat boots were needed by the Army.[8] Silk became nearly impossible to buy because it was used in making parachutes for the armed forces. Home front rationing also included gasoline and rubber. Rubber was another of the first products to be rationed. Prior to the outbreak of hostilities, 97 percent of the nation's crude rubber came from Southeast Asia, from Indonesia and Malaysia. By 1942, the Japanese had conquered these countries and controlled the southeastern Pacific sea lanes. They gobbled up almost all of the nation's crude rubber supply. Americans were asked to conduct rubber drives and such items as old overshoes, hot water bottles and beach balls were turned in at the nearest collection centers located at gas stations. These collections did little good because most items were made of reclaimed rubber and were useful for making floor mats but not for making tires. The rationing of rubber meant the rationing of tires. Motorists were required to register their tires and turn in excess ones. Recapping and retreading of used tires was not a satisfactory solution to the tire shortage. The first efforts to make synthetic rubber were not successful. Inner tubes usually contained several patches as punctures were a frequent occurrence. Under the headline "How to Save on Tires," in a 1942 edition of the *Argus Leader*, an article pictured Hollywood actress Alexis Smith behind the steering wheel of a car. An empty milk bottle stood next to her on the floorboard. The picture's purpose was "to show when you are driving too fast the bottle would tip over; at patriotic speeds, which saved on tires the bottle stays upright."[9] Later in the war, the United States began to import some rubber from Brazil, where the rubber industry was still in its nascent state. There was a freeze, therefore, on auto and truck tires and a ban on recapping tires. By this time, the American Navy had substantially reduced the threat from German submarines.

In May 1942, gas was being rationed on the East Coast of the United States. The shortage of fuel was caused by the large number of tankers being sunk by German submarines in the Atlantic Ocean. Gas rationing for the entire nation went into effect on December 1, 1942. In January 1943, President Roosevelt ordered a ban on pleasure driving and a thirty-five-miles-per-hour speed limit on all highways. Much of the available gasoline was being directed to military operations. Every motorist had a sticker on the windshield of his vehicle with the appropriate letter of priority from A to E and T. People with an A sticker had the lowest gasoline allocation. They were allotted four (later three) gallons per week. If you drove your car only for pleasure your windshield had an A sticker. Nationwide, the quantities of gasoline rationed varied by region from time to time. Commuters working in a war industry or driving in a car pool received a B sticker and these car owners received an amount of gasoline based on their distance from work. Police and clergy autos displayed an E, or emergency, sticker. People in this category, physicians, clergy, police, etc., could purchase as many gallons of gasoline as needed to carry out their duties. One OPA estimate indicated that nearly half of all American drivers had B and C stickers. Truckers were given a T sticker, which granted them permission to obtain all of the gas they needed. Gasoline and tire rationing gave rise to a black market in large urban centers. A part of this was the theft of gasoline coupons and the counterfeiting of the coupons.[10]

The tire and gasoline shortage ended store-to-home deliveries. Housewives found that shopping by phone was a thing of the past. With the restrictions on gasoline and tires, trains became the primary way to travel any distance. There were very few tourists on trains. The passengers were soldiers on leave, soldiers' wives joining their husbands in the military and the hundreds of troop trains moving thousands of men to new assignments, usually to departure ports on the Atlantic and Pacific coasts.

Local farmers also experienced the impact of rationing. The South Dakota Department of Agriculture War Board ordered county farm machinery committees to begin rationing new farm machinery and equipment. Because farm products were as desperately needed as those of industry, several banks, including Northwest Security National Bank, offered farmers "Victory Loans." Using the available media, they proclaimed, "Don't let your farms go into slack production for want of funds."[11] If a farmer's binder, threshing machine, tractor or plow broke down and spare parts were not available, farmers often turned to the area blacksmith to shape a suitable replacement. With the draft, many farm boys were called into the armed services. In some cases, a single son was given a deferment. Many farm women undertook tasks previously held by men. They drove tractors, did the milking, operated the cream separator and fed the hogs and chickens. Many threshing crews employed a "machine man" whose sole task was to keep tractors and threshing machines in working order.

Farmers were granted unlimited amounts of gasoline but only after filling out the paperwork required by the OPA. Some city dwellers suspected, but could not prove, that there were farmers who used "machinery designated gasoline" for their automobiles. Certainly, black market practices were not as prevalent in rural areas as they were in the urban trucking industry.

## "MAKING DO"

Local citizens, particularly housewives, learned to make do in meeting the challenges created by rationing and shortages. They learned how to bake eggless and sugarless cakes. Many adhered to the government's plea for "meatless Tuesdays." Fantle's Department Store advertised rayon stockings for women indicating that "Silk and Nylon have gone to war." Some women resorted to leg makeup rather than wear the old fashioned rayon stockings. It had been customary during the Great Depression for young people who developed a hole in the sole of their shoes to shape cardboard to cover the hole. With a shortage of shoes during World War II, cardboard continued to be a quick fix if there were no shoe repair shops in the area. Being a cooperative neighbor was essential. One family borrowed a gasoline ration book from their neighbors so they had enough fuel to drive thirty-five miles to a funeral.[12] Ration stamps were distributed by local rationing boards, usually located in grade schools and staffed by teachers and volunteers.

The manufacture of electrical appliances, jewelry, woolen goods, and even clocks was at a standstill for civilians. Lil Norlin gave the wife of a GI stationed at the ATS an alarm clock. Her husband had to be awake by 5:00 A.M. in order not to be late for school at the base.[13] It was during the war that daylight savings time was introduced. Taxes also increased as 10 percent was taken from payrolls.[14]There was a black market of people who were willing to pay enough to buy items without ration coupons. Historians have estimated that on the national level 25 percent of all retail business was conducted on the black market. There was some subterfuge on the local level. In Sioux Falls, with its large North European population, there was always a demand for coffee, one of the scarce commodities during the war. There was an informal code a citizen could use at one local grocery store. The customer would ask, "Could I have some food for my canary?" The clerk would respond, "Does your canary drip or perk?" Then he would look under the counter to see what coffee was available. On rare occasions, nylons and cigarettes came to stores. They, too, were hidden under the counter and sold only to select customers.[15] The great majority of the city's population was very patriotic and frowned on such practices. They adhered to the popular slogan, "Use it up, wear it out, make it do or do without."

## PATRIOTIC PRACTICES

The civilian population did more than provide hungry soldiers with home-cooked chicken dinners. The people of Sioux Falls and those in other communities participated in volunteer work, conducted salvage drives and planted and cared for "Victory Gardens." Victory Gardens were probably the most popular of the civilian war effort tasks. They combined recreation and patriotism. Whole families spent Saturday working in their gardens. Housewives revived the nearly lost art of canning, putting up part of the family crop at harvest time. The number of gardens quickly declined at the end of the war. People found the convenience of the super-market preferable.

Adults and children conducted salvage drives, collecting scrap iron, waste paper, rags, rubber products, tin cans, batteries and old tires. Children contributed the tin foil off gum wrappers, and adults turned in toothpaste tubes when they purchased a new one. Housewives turned in bacon grease and other fats that contained glycerin that was used in the making of ammunition. Rural school children picked milkweed pods after they were ripe. The pods were fed to silkworms that made silk used in the production of parachutes.[16] Farmers brought machinery they no longer used to railroad loading docks. These rusted and weathered implements were located in pastures, farmyards or groves of trees.[17] From Sioux Falls this scrap iron was transported to production centers in the industrial Midwest and used in the manufacturing of armored tanks, artillery and other forms of weaponry.

There were savings bond drives highlighted by parades on Phillips Avenue featuring troops and musicians from the Army Technical School. School children purchased war bond stamps for twenty-five cents per week. They glued the stamps into made-to-order booklets. When a book was filled, they would take it to a local bank and receive a savings bond. Families with a son or daughter in military service hung a rectangular banner in the window that had a blue star in the center against a white and red background. There was a blue star for each young person who had heeded the nation's call to arms. A gold star replaced a blue one with the death of a son or daughter on active duty overseas.

Participation in community volunteer work took many forms. Girl Scout troops spent hours folding bandages for the Red Cross. Some women did knitting or sewing for the servicemen. Young women cleaned houses and babysat for women who worked at the ATS.[18] Local churches prepared mimeographed newsletters that were sent to servicemen who belonged to their congregation. East Side Lutheran Church compiled one of the more comprehensive newsletters. First Lutheran Church established a USO-type hostelry in the lower level of the church. Other churches held open-house activities in their recreation areas or lounges.

The Office of War Information (OWI) provided large colored patriotic posters for area postmasters to place on the walls of their respective lobbies. The posters reminded local citizens of the war and their duties. The Japanese were portrayed with protruding front teeth and were accompanied in large letters by the slogan, "Slap the Jap with Scrap." With appropriate pictorial background, others read, "Loose Lips Sink Ships" and "Our Flag, Love It Or Leave It."

## ENTERTAINMENT

Reading remained a basic form of entertainment for many soldiers and the citizens of Sioux Falls. Many servicemen came to the public library wanting books on radio, physics, and mathematics. According to the librarian, Alberta Caille, "We always have from 3 to 15 boys in the library and Sunday seems like open house." They checked out works of fiction, but when they did their tastes were similar to those of the civilian population. Among the favorite books that were checked out were Lloyd Douglas' *The Robe*, Ben Ames Williams' *Stranger Women*, and Bess Streeter Aldrich's *The Lieutenant's Lady*. Soldiers' wives spent little time in the library but there were always requests for entertainment and cookbooks.[19]

Radio serials, providing entertainment for children after school, dramatized their heroes, such as Captain Midnight, Superman and Jack Armstrong, the All-American Boy, who were involved in struggles with the Nazis or Japanese. Comic strips featuring Joe Palooka and Terry and the Pirates concentrated on the war. In the evening, adults could listen to Gabriel Heater who always introduced his newscast with, "There is good (or bad) news this evening." They also could listen to Edward R. Murrow reporting from London, England. Families always looked forward to comedies and there were many to choose from including *Fibber McGee and Mollie* and *The Bob Hope Show*, with Hope usually presenting his program at a military installation and the wooden dummy Charlie McCarthy matching wits with bald-headed Edgar Bergen. It was through radio that Kate Smith popularized *God Bless America*.

The nickelodeon or jukebox, which played a record when one inserted a nickel in the slot, in addition to the Big Band sound, played a number of songs reflecting the on-going conflict in Asia and Europe. Among the records played were "Praise the Lord and Pass the Ammunition," "The White Cliffs of Dover," "Coming in On a Wing and a Prayer," "Don't Sit Under the Apple Tree with Anyone Else but Me," "They're Either Too Young Or Too Old," "Don't Get Around Much Anymore," "I'll Walk Alone," and "Saturday Night Is the Loneliest Night of the Week."

Per capita income increased dramatically during the first half of the 1940s. The local citizenry had money to spend for entertainment outside of the home. They had to compete, however, with the many GIs enjoying a day of "liberty" in the city. There were five theaters in Sioux Falls in 1942: the Egyptian, Granada, Hollywood, Orpheum and State theaters. Many of the movies contained war themes and featured male actors whose theatrical careers thrived during the ensuing decades. Dana Andrews starred in *A Walk in the Sun*, Robert Mitchum in *Aerial Gunner*, Randolph Scott in *Gung Ho*, Richard Arlen in *Submarine Alert*, Ronald Reagan in *Flight Patrol* and *International Squadron*, Bud Abbott and Lou Costello in *Buck Private,* and Robert Taylor in *Bataan*.

If one was fortunate enough to secure a reservation several days in advance, a couple or a family could enjoy a meal or snack at the Chocolate Shop, 106 South Phillips, which advertised itself as "adventures in good eating," the Palace of Sweets, 301 South Phillips, and the Town 'n Country café on West 12th Street. Other opportunities for eating out were the Cove Tea Room, the popular Shriver Johnson Tea Room, the Manhattan Café, the China Café at 124 South Main Avenue, the Nickel Plate and the venerable Hamburger Inn. Soldiers crowded the counters at Sioux Falls cafes. Cafes had to make do with many shortages including help, cooking oils and shortening. They also had to contend with meat and coffee rationing and as the war went on it was almost impossible to get canned goods.[20] If a customer needed a libation, the city had thirty-six on-sale liquor establishments, twenty-two of them located on Main and Phillips Avenues.[21]

Dancing was the primary form of adult entertainment during the Great Depression and World War II. Two types of music had emerged from the 1920s. Jazz had become popular in the South while "sweet music," characterized by an unobtrusive beat and a quieter sound, exemplified by Guy Lombardo and the Royal Canadians, was popular in the ballrooms of the northern states.

After experimentation, Benny Goodman and his band introduced the classical period of jazz, 1935-1945. Saxophones and clarinets were added to accompany trumpets, trombones and rhythm sections. The tuba was replaced by the string bass and the guitar took the place of the banjo. The big bands, striving for the ensemble sound, stayed together during most of the war years.

People in the coastal states and Chicago were not the only ones to benefit from the presence of the big bands and their vitality. The one-night stands of these bands became popular in the Midwest and Northern Plains. Jan Garber introduced a form of performance schedule that flourished during the war years. His band was offered the chance to play in San Francisco but he knew that traveling from Chicago to San Francisco would take more money than the band would make in San Francisco. Garber pioneered the cross-country tour, playing in smaller cities for one night to finance the whole trip. Other big bands copied his tactics, bringing swing music to people dancing in ballrooms instead of listening to the music through the radios in their living rooms. Mag Hansen, who managed the Arkota Ballroom in downtown Sioux Falls, said the big bands "really packed them in."[22] All the big bands played the Arkota at one time or another along with other ballrooms in adjacent states. Among the bands was Tommy Dorsey's sweet band with a young vocalist named Frank Sinatra. Louis Armstrong and his band appeared at the Arkota as well as Vaughn Monroe and his thirty-three-piece band. Lawrence Welk and his Hotsy Totsy Band, which appeared regularly on WNAX radio, Yankton, South Dakota, played their first dance at the Arkota. While in Sioux Falls, these bands usually made an appearance at the ATS to entertain the servicemen.

While most local people came to the Arkota to dance, others came just to listen to musicians who had a national reputation. Hansen often found people, twenty rows deep, watching a musician like Charley Shavers, a trumpet player in the Dorsey Brothers band, who brought his own personal valet to the ballroom. Four nights a week the ballroom was open to dancing with admission fixed at 75 cents. When a name band played, the admission charge was $1.50.[23]

Several of the big bands began to break up before the end of World War II. Band leaders along with band members were drafted into military service. Glenn Miller, perhaps the most notable band leader, lost his life while entertaining the troops in Western Europe. By the 1950s, the remaining bands had converted to more popular music and less good dance music. Mag Hansen indicated that in the post-World War period very few nationally renowned big bands played the Arkota. The big bands that still existed confined their engagements primarily to the West Coast and to Las Vegas. Small, local bands would play infrequently at the Arkota, but the old dance music no longer reverberated off the walls of the venerable ballroom.[24]

## RAILROADS

The Japanese attack on Pearl Harbor resulted in the greatest movement of men and supplies known in world history. Day and night, somewhere in the United States, a special troop movement started every six minutes. A freight train, loaded with vital war goods and foodstuffs, high-balled out of a make-up yard every four seconds.[25]

Railroads played a significant role in Sioux Falls during World War II. The train track was the artery of economic and social life and the depot was its heart. If one were asked, aside from the family, what were the most important institutions in a community located in the Northern Plains, the standard response would be the school and the church. The railroad depot should be added to the list. The station agent was just as important as the local school superintendent and the pastors and priests. Sioux Falls was fortunate to have been served by five different railroad companies.

Playing a dominant role in the transport of troops to and from the Army Technical School was the Chicago, Milwaukee & St. Paul Railroad, with its depot located at 501 North Phillips Avenue.

The agent at the Milwaukee depot was Lloyd F. West, who served as coordinator for troop movements through his contacts with the Western Military Bureau in Chicago. West was notified by the authorities at the ATS when a contingent of men was leaving the base and their first destination. If more than 125 GIs were involved, the designation "Special Train" was used. If it was a "Special Train," West contacted transportation authorities in Washington, D.C., to secure a special number for the train. After he received the number, West passed it on to the other agents along the railroad line. To handle the extra work, the military sent additional men from Detroit, Michigan, to assist the agent.[26] During the war, railroad work did not allow holidays, Sundays or days off for personnel because of the continuing process of moving passengers and troops in and out of Sioux Falls. Normally, two clerks were assigned to the depot but during the war there were eight clerks.[27]

Depot agents also served as local agents for Western Union. During the war, these agents had the unpleasant task of delivering telegrams from the War Department that contained bad news for several area families with sons serving in the military overseas. Parents were informed if their sons had been killed in action, wounded, or were missing in action. As the war intensified in Europe following D-Day and in the Pacific after the adoption of the "island hopping" campaign, the number of telegrams increased.

Although the citizens of Sioux Falls did without many things, they never experienced the extreme hardships that civilians living in war zones endured. Local residents contended with shortages and government controls, but they understood there had to be sacrifice in pursuit of victory. Knowing what had to be done engendered a communal spirit in support of the war effort.

When the war ended, people wondered, "What now?" In their first efforts to restore daily life, they still contended with many shortages. They envisioned buying a new car to replace their "Old Faithful," which had limited use during the war. At the war's end, long lines appeared at gas pumps, despite the need for new tires. People dreamed of steaks, nylons, new housing, and abundant coffee and sugar—all of the food and technology they had been denied since 1942-43. The population had accrued savings and war bonds and they were eager to purchase products they had been denied because of the Great Depression and wartime shortages. Their first thoughts, however, were given over to bringing the men and women of the armed forces home and the termination of government controls over housing and rationing.

# Chapter 12

## VICTORY AND DRAW DOWN

*Lines at Christmas fret me*
*Movie lines upset me.*
*But a line I will gladly sweat out*
*Is when I'm finally let out.*
*– Sioux Sentinel, September 28, 1945*

*Fellas, There's no more flak.*
*Never again, any more flak.*
*– An unidentified lieutenant*

What was most likely in the future for a graduate of the Army Technical School in 1943-1944? He would be transferred to gunnery school, usually the school at Yuma, Arizona. From there, almost all of them became part of the 8th Air Force based in England. The radio operator became part of a ten-man crew aboard a B-17 Flying Fortress. The other nine members of the crew were the pilot and co-pilot, bombardier, navigator, flight engineer and four gunners. In a combat situation, all of the men except the pilot and co-pilot served as gunners. During their first time in combat, the gunners had never practiced from a moving aircraft, and a number of the radio operators were still unfamiliar with the Morse code.

In an agreement with the British, the Americans would bomb enemy targets during the daylight hours while the British engaged in night bombing. The 8th Air Force suffered major losses as they bombed targets in France and Germany. American pilots flew their B-17s in a massed formation of twelve or more planes. Using this formation, they hoped to bring collective firepower against an attacker. Unfortunately, on their flights over Germany they were constantly attacked by German fighter aircraft in the sky and flak from anti-aircraft fire from the ground.

On August 17, 1943, 376 Flying Fortresses were sent deep into Germany to attack crucial military facilities in Regensburg and Schweinfurt. The Messerschmitt 109 was manufactured at Regensburg with ball bearings produced in Schweinfurt. Both sites were well beyond the range of U.S. fighter aircraft. It was a devastating day for American airmen, including the radio operators. Sixty bombers were shot down and forty-seven others were so badly damaged that they had to be scrapped. Many of the radio operators had taken their training at the Sioux Falls base. Soon after this costly raid, their obituaries began to appear in the *Polar Tech*. The demand for new aircraft crews, including radio operators trained in Sioux Falls, reached its peak before D-Day. Around-the-clock bombing of German sites continued but further raids deep into Germany were limited until the B-17s could be escorted by American fighter planes. During 1944, the 8th Air Force lost 2,400 Flying Fortresses.

Fighter planes were modified: the P-47 Thunderbolt and the P-3l Lightning were equipped with drop tanks, external auxiliary fuel tanks that enabled them to accompany the Flying Fortresses further into Germany. The most outstanding American fighter plane, the P-51 Mustang, was continually modified in 1943. The Mustang had a larger fuel capacity and was powered by a Rolls Royce Merlin engine. The aircraft had 108-gallon auxiliary fuel tanks under each wing that could be jettisoned when empty. The P-51 was a heavy, long-range fighter aircraft with the performance of a short-range interceptor. The United States would build 14,000 of these invaluable weapons. With its high speed and long-range, the Mustang could escort bombers all the way to Berlin and return to bases in England or French territory, which had been liberated following D-Day, June 6, 1944. The German air force was destroyed not only in the air but also on the ground. Using tactics earlier employed by the Germans, Allied fighter planes engaged the enemy in the air and fighter aircraft bombed and strafed hangars, maintenance revetments and planes on the ground. Among the most effective fighter aircraft during strafing missions was the Republic P-47 Thunderbolt.[1] In the air war against the Germans, 79,265 American airmen lost their lives.

By March 7, 1945, the Third Reich was dying. Germany had irremediably lost the war in Europe and was absorbing the worst defeat that ever had been inflicted upon a major nation in modern times. In March, spearheads of the U. S. 9th Armored Division

Listening to the public address loudspeaker announce a celebration of V-E Day. Students were excused fifteen minutes early to hear the program. *Center for Western Studies.*

crossed the Rhine River at Remagen. Patton's 3rd Army established another beachhead across the Rhine near Oppenheim. The U. S. 9th Army made contact with the Russian Army coming from the east at the Elbe River on April 11. The Elbe had been designated the previous year as the demarcation line between the Soviet and Western occupation zones in Germany. The capture of Berlin was left to the Red Army. On April 21, Soviet tanks entered the northern suburbs of Berlin. The war in Europe was drawing to a close. On May 7-8, the Germans signed a general surrender of their armed forces at General Eisenhower's headquarters at Rheims in France. When hearing news of Victory in Europe (V-E) Day, there were no spontaneous demonstrations among the GIs stationed at the Sioux

Falls Army Technical School. The event was anti-climactic. The German defeat was expected—but they still had to win the war in the Pacific. There was heartfelt relief that the war was over in Europe. Nevertheless, additional MPs as well as fifteen police officers were assigned to patrol hotels, depots and streets. It was unnecessary. No soldiers were picked up for disorderly conduct. There was not a single instance of poor discipline.[2]

With the war in Europe drawing to an end, rapid and significant changes occurred at the Sioux Falls Army Technical School. On March 16, 1945, Colonel Raymond J. Reeves succeeded Colonel Oscar L. Rogers as the base commander. Rogers, who had been in command since August 1943, for seventeen months, left for Washington, D.C., to attend a seminar for staff officers.[3] Reeves was the first of eight men who were assigned to command the Sioux Falls ATS until it closed.[4] (See Chapter 3.)

At the end of March 1945, orders arrived from St. Louis that no new classes would begin at the school until further notice. Class 435 was the last to enter the school. The class commenced training on April 6.[5] There was a temporary surplus of radio operator-mechanics piling up at gunnery schools because of the end of large-scale aerial operations in Europe. It was announced that the Sioux Falls Air Base would become a redeployment center. Air Force veterans from the European Theater of Operations (ETO) would be ordered to Sioux Falls after a thirty-day furlough for advanced training before being transferred to the Pacific Theater of Operations. As many as 65,000 overseas veterans with combat service were assigned to ATS schools with 1,300 of them in the first contingent sent to the Sioux Falls base.[6] At the Sioux Falls base, all branches of the Air Force would take a refresher course that included new knowledge of up-to-the-minute retraining devices and methods of air combat using B-29s, the super Flying Fortresses, the aerial weapon of choice in the Pacific theater.[7] The mission of the Sioux Falls installation changed almost overnight.

## RADIO TRAINING ENDS

In May 1945, it was announced that the Army Air Forces Training Command Radio School, operative since July 6, 1942, would soon be closed. Official word arrived that the base would be taken over on June 1 by the 2nd Air Force and that it would serve as a redeployment center for air crews being transferred from the ETO to the war in the Pacific. The last classes of radio operators to receive their diplomas graduated on May 11. More than 45,000 radio operator-mechanics (ROMs) flowed through the base from July 6, 1942, to May 11, 1945. One-hundred and sixty-one classes had entered the program and 139 graduated or completed the course. It was estimated that in the European Theater of Operations more than 50 percent of the ROMs were graduates of the Sioux Falls ATS. In mid-summer 1944, the base newspaper continued to state, as noted earlier, that the Sioux Falls ATS was generally recognized as the Number One AAF Radio School of its type in the United States.[8]

## REDEPLOYMENT

On June 1, all military personnel with the exception of radio instructors, students, aircraft maintenance men and certain administrative personnel were transferred to the 2nd Air Force. All of the base aircraft were to be removed and reassigned to the Eastern Technical Training Command.[9] The first batch of ETO veterans arrived on June 29; the new arrivals, 150 officers and enlisted men were from the 15th Air Force. Men over thirty-eight years of age or who had earned eighty points or more were granted the option of volunteering for further service against the Japanese or remaining in the United States on Permanent Party assignments.[10]

An accident away from the base caused a brief interruption in a well-organized redeployment procedure. A twin engine B-25 had been added to the base fleet. Christened "Old John Feather Merchant," the bomber was to serve as a ferry plane. On July 28, 1945, the plane was returning to the base in Sioux Falls from the East Coast when the pilot became lost in a dense fog. Traveling at 200 miles an hour, the twelve-ton bomber slammed into the 78th floor of New York City's Empire State building, 975 feet above street level. The plane's aviation fuel exploded unleashing a fireball inside the skyscraper. The plane's three occupants and eleven people in the building were killed. The Army responded to the crash by requiring more intensive transitional training for pilots returning from overseas combat duty.[11]

By the end of July, the Sioux Falls air base had become a central assembly station for units being redeployed. During the month, over 20,000 men had been processed but due to deficiencies in transportation only 6,382 had been shipped out. In August, more than 30,000 additional men were received at the overworked and understaffed base. During the first week in September, it was announced that the 50,000th man had been processed through Sioux Falls.[12]

The pace at the base was frantic. A Strategic Air Command historian wrote, "If Sioux Falls wasn't the busiest army air field in the United States during redeployment, it certainly was one of the most chaotic." "Organized Confusion" was a term frequently and aptly applied to the situation by base personnel."[13]

## A RAUCOUS CELEBRATION

On Tuesday, August 14, at 6:00 P.M., Central War Time, President Harry Truman announced via radio that the Japanese had accepted surrender terms. The *Argus Leader* flashed the joyous news on its external neon lightboard and began preparing an extra edition of the paper. Whistles at Sioux Falls' industrial sites started blowing at 6:15 P.M. and thousands of people began to jam Phillips Avenue on a beautiful August evening. Some people described the gathering as Sioux Falls' largest and most emotional celebration.

Thousands of GIs from the air base, dressed in their sun-tans, led the raucous celebration. The pandemonium began on Phillips Avenue in the 200 block near 11th Street. Most of the men had been overseas and were in Sioux Falls awaiting redeployment to the Pacific Theater of War when news of Japan's surrender spread like wildfire throughout the base. Many of the men were tired of sitting around the base, beset with boredom.[14] Joined by hundreds of civilians, the soldiers packed Phillips Avenue between 10th and 11th streets from curb to curb.

Hordes of GIs cut off each other's neckties. The airmen led many in a snake dance. Veterans and civilians threw paper streamers and hurled confetti. With traffic on Phillips Avenue at a standstill, drivers sounded their car horns, contributing to a deafening background that included cheering, singing and shouting. Packed buses and cars were rocked. A sixty-three-year-old man was killed when hit by a car. A photographer for *YANK* magazine said, "It looks as though America has been liberated."[15] A lieutenant, wearing pilot's wings, and several rows of ribbons, jumped up on a car's running board and held up his hand for order. "Fellas," he said, "There's no more flak. Never again, any more flak." He, of course, referred to the anti-aircraft fire that flight crews encountered during combat. After brief silence from his buddies, the merriment resumed.

There were other impromptu speeches and GIs pounded each other on the back. Airmen put on civilian hats, neckties and other articles of clothing given to them by residents of Sioux Falls.

Amidst all of the frivolity, a considerable amount of liquor was consumed and acts of vandalism occurred.[16] Jerry W. Whiting reported that several of the policemen were drinking and that crowd control was useless. A group of GIs found a bus driver to take them to The Plaza, a club outside of the city. The bus stopped on the way as the bus driver decided he was too drunk to drive any further.[17] A group of soldiers overturned a Model-T Ford at 10th and Phillips and set it on fire. The GIs seized the fire truck that soon arrived, grabbed the hoses and hand extinguishers and put out the fire. They then turned the hose on shrieking bystanders. The city fire chief stated that several pieces of equipment were missing when the truck returned to Central Fire Station. Other airmen pulled call levers causing false fire alarms. They opened a fire hydrant at 11th and Phillips Avenue. Small geysers were created when they broke off drinking fountains at 8th and Phillips and 11th and Phillips. Six store windows were smashed and one awning was set on fire. There was a lot of hugging and kissing.

Mrs. Paul Graves and another woman were on their way to the 806 Club when a GI grabbed her arm. In anger, she shouted, "What are you doing?" A few minutes later, a bottle cleared her head and went through a plate-glass window.[18] Display windows were broken at a half-dozen downtown stores. A tall, blonde woman, accompanying an Air Force captain, shouted, "Bombs away!" as she hurled a bottle at E.C. Olson's clothing store window. The bottle was the only thing that broke. A military policeman said quietly, "You shouldn't be doing things like that."

Other hi-jinx included two GIs loading seven of their fellow airmen into a contractor's rubber-tired wheel barrow and pushing them down the center of Phillips Avenue. Other soldiers commandeered a three-ton truck and drove it slowly along Phillips Avenue. They shouted, sang snatches of songs and lifted women standing along the route into the truck.  The riders broke open countless cartons of cigarettes as they cruised slowly down the avenue and threw hundreds of packs into the shouting mass of people who scrambled for the precious items.  For civilians, it was probably the last time they would have to hustle for cigarettes.  Ted Ramsey, of the *Argus Leader*, said, "A good place to stay away from was downtown." Yet Ramsey had a different assessment of what took place than did other observers.  He wrote that no one was hurt seriously.  There had been a few minor incidents.  And, yes, one car was turned over and burned but there was very little vandalism.[19]  He made no mention of one man being struck and killed by an automobile.

During the evening, Army medics stood by at military police headquarters in city hall ready to give first aid to GIs injured in fights, falls or accidents. Twenty extra policemen and 200 MPs were called out before a 1:30 A.M. curfew silenced the demonstrators.[20] A significant number of soldiers were hauled into the bullpen at the police station.  They were then relayed by bus to the guardhouse at the base.  While the celebration went on along Phillips Avenue, there was no levity at the base.  The night shift of GIs and civilian workers remained at their jobs, keeping busy processing thousands of men for redeployment or reassignment.[21]

In early September, the long-standing curfew was lifted for all personnel as long as discipline and conduct of troops remained at a high level.  All transient personnel were required to meet morning formations.[22]

## A DISCHARGE CENTER

Following the formal surrender of the Japanese on September 2, it was announced that the former Army Technical School would undergo another change.  It became a separation (discharge) center on Monday, September 17.  Sioux Falls was one of thirty-two specially created Army Air Forces centers established to speed the return of men with high service point totals back to civilian life.  Nationwide, the government expected to release 1,300,000 men by Christmas. The overall plan was to demobilize five million men within a year. The eligible age limit was reduced from forty to thirty-eight.  Using a service point system, men who had accumulated at least eighty-five service points, and WACs who had accumulated forty-four points, would be discharged first. The men received one point for each month of service since September 16, 1940. They also received one point for each month overseas since September 16, 1940, five points for each combat decoration (battle participation stars), and twelve points for each child under ten years of age up to a limit of three children.[23] One of the first men to be discharged was Edward M. Scribner, a self-taught engineer who had designed the base's broadcasting system.[24] One airman with 160 missions over Occupied Europe had acquired 267 points toward discharge. As separation proceeded, the number of needed points was revised downwards.[25]

As personnel at the base developed more expeditious ways of handling records, the Separation Center increased the tempo. By September 28, 400 officers and enlisted men were discharged in a single day. When the discharge center shifted to a six-day week, men were separated from the service thirty hours after their arrival in Sioux Falls. As of October 26, 10,000 men had been discharged at the air base, and the separation of Permanent Party personnel also had begun. The original schedule had men becoming ex-GIs on their fifth day at the base. During day one, they heard a talk on the GI Bill of Rights, the Veterans Administration, the Red Cross, the U.S. Employment Service and educational possibilities as they adapted to civilian life. The Information and Education Branch of Personnel Services was conducting classes in vocational and academic subjects. One could get hours toward a high school or college diploma. Courses would be taken on a voluntary basis. The base machine shop was open to men who might be interested in welding, sheet metal work and home refrigeration.[26] Full credit was also being offered through Augustana College and Washington High School in Sioux Falls. College courses would be designed for a person to earn a quarter credit by concentrating on a subject for three weeks. At the college, credit could be obtained in freshman mathematics, trigonometry, algebra, history and English.[27]

The GIs were alerted to the fact that their first civilian suit would cost between $30 and $40.[28] They also learned the details of one of the most significant pieces of legislation in U.S. history. The Servicemen's Readjustment Act of 1944, signed by President Franklin D. Roosevelt on June 22, 1944, enabled a whole generation of young men to obtain a college education or technical training. The "GI Bill of Rights" provided subsistence allowance, tuition, fees, and books and supplies for the education of veterans of World War II. The average cost of a college education in 1945 was $900. Over one million men and women enrolled in colleges and universities in 1946. Almost one out of every two students who enrolled was a veteran. The former GIs considered higher education as the key to upward mobility—and they dominated the honor rolls and dean's lists. The same legislation provided other demobilized veterans with loans to start new businesses and subsidies to acquire new skills.[29]

On their second day at the base, men to be discharged checked in at Supply and turned in overages and issue shortages in the basic issue with which they left for civilian life. On the third day, they had a medical exam and were counseled individually. On the fourth day, they signed forms previously typed by the office personnel and, as indicated, on the fifth day they became ex-GIs.[30]

In late October, Brigadier General Robert F. Travis announced that the air base would become inactive on December 31, 1945.[31] All separations at the base ended on Sunday, November 25, with the discharge of the 18,985th man. The process had begun on September 19 with ninety men being discharged. As the base began to shut down, remaining aircraft were transferred to other air bases. Aircraft being relocated included AT-11s, four C-46s, two AT-6s, one C-64 and one B-25.[32]

Beginning in November 1945, publication of the *Sioux Sentinel* was reduced to a small tabloid in size of only five pages. There was a lack of trained personnel to report the news and prepare for its publication. The newspaper published its final edition on November 30, 1945.[33] The first edition of the *Polar Tech* had been issued to the GIs on August 21, 1942. The 2nd Air Command continued with gradual demobilization and evacuation until December 31, 1945, when the facilities were officially deactivated. Military strength at the base had peaked on July 31, 1945, with an official count of 27,854 men and women.[34] At the end of November 1945, the base hospital had only eighty-five patients as the consolidation of medical facilities continued. It was closed on December 26. The AAF Regional Station Hospital was still admitting patients at the end of November. Many were orthopedic patients undergoing rehabilitation.[35] A dispensary at the base handled emergency cases and minor respiratory disease cases.

The USO club at 11th and Main Avenue closed on December 15, while the other club at 9th and Dakota Avenue remained open until January 15, 1946, serving the skeleton crew of 1,055 still at the airfield. The last of the line of commanding officers, Colonel Phillip Foote, arrived and departed in the two weeks prior to deactivation. The small number of German POWs, taken prisoner during the North African Campaign, 1942-43, who had been held in the southeast area of the base, near the barracks of the black soldiers and the base's coal supply, were transferred to Algona, Iowa, to prepare for repatriation to Germany. The 350 former members of General Rommel's Afrika Corps had worked in the warehouses and in base maintenance.[36] The swimming pool at Terrace Park was given to the city, and only two buses, using the main Gate 2 facing Prairie Avenue, brought passengers to and from the base.[37]

As the base officially closed, Lieutenant Joseph Nichols, at first sent to the base for redeployment, received orders to stay on as the surplus property officer. As of June 1946, he was the only Army representative at the base. Working in conjunction with the War Assets Administration (WAA), he was responsible for the custody and shipment of surplus property sold by the WAA. As he walked out the gate for the last time, a significant chapter in the history of Sioux Falls came to an end.[38]

## A BASE FOR SALE

Originally, about 950 units of various kinds were built at the Army Technical School. The War Assets Administration sold 455 surplus frame structures to private buyers. Many were to be used for school buildings and veterans' housing. With base liquidation, the city of Sioux Falls sold the approximately 110 buildings (with utilities acquired) at the termination of the federal government's lease.[39]

The airport became one of the major benefactors with the closure of the base. In addition to buildings, the ATS left a sewage plant, railroad facilities, roads, runways and an electric substation. The Big Sioux River channel was changed to make room for an expanded runway complex. The total cost of all these government projects was more than $12 million.

The city sold three warehouses netting $43,586. A week earlier, Sioux Falls sold seventy barracks and other buildings for $31,115.

The city had eighteen former Army warehouses and thirty-six plots, including the building sites.[40] The city set minimum bids on some of the remaining buildings. Thirty-six barracks were appraised at $300 each, eight latrines at $240 each, and eight day rooms at $260 each. The highest bid received for a barrack was $485, for a latrine $727.50 and for a dayroom $260.[41]

Several buildings, particularly the warehouses, became part of the city's first industrial park. They contained materials to be distributed and sold in southeastern South Dakota. A few of the barracks were moved to local college campuses to be used to house the influx of World War II veterans using the GI Bill. A large classroom building became a temporary natural science center at Augustana College. One wing of the building became a small theater where dramatic productions were staged. Another structure was converted into an art building, which was in use on the campus until the 1990s. A theater building and two barracks were moved to the junior college in Freeman. A mess hall was dismantled by members of First Reformed Church for a new church at 19th Street and Grange Avenue. Two of the base chapels became the sites of new congregations. One of them became the first site of Our Savior's Lutheran Church. The other was located in southeast Sioux Falls for a new Catholic congregation. The city established a temporary day camp for neighborhood children in one of the base structures. Within the building, children were taught arts and crafts, played games and performed plays that often were products of their imagination or based on stories that they had read.[42] Outside of the building an area was made suitable for the youngsters to play basketball. Other buildings were dismantled and the lumber used for construction purposes in different parts of the city.[43]

## ECONOMIC AND SOCIAL CHANGE

The air base brought financial prosperity and social change. Sioux Falls would never again be the isolated, agricultural community it had once been. The Army Technical School made an indelible economic and social impact, stimulating growth and change. The ATS was responsible for creating many jobs and a multi-million-dollar monthly payroll for the city. The Army intensified its recruitment of men in 1944 with the impending invasion of Europe on June 6. Their departure led to the hiring of many more civilian men and women to work on the base or in the hospitals. Civilian contractors provided services to the military throughout the war. The contractors were kept busy with expansion and repair projects. The Army Technical School also hired civilians for many technical jobs. Civilian pay per year ranged between $1,620 and $4,600. When federal contracts and payments came to an end after January 1, 1946, the city's leadership believed that Sioux Falls had a greater economic destiny than its current status as a mixed industrial and agricultural economy.

A building boom occurred. It was the beginning of one of the biggest building and expansion eras in the city's history. Judee Koplow Epstein, a local woman who worked in the Message Center, speaking about the base and radio school, said, "It made Sioux Falls. The economic impact was phenomenal. Everybody made money. People who were in dire straits before all of a sudden were very affluent."[44] The war left Sioux Falls with growing pains, as the population now

An Army Technical School building being used to house the Art Department on the campus of Augustana College in 1969.

stood at 52,161. The city started to expand with the construction of hundreds of new homes, but a housing shortage still persisted. A major building project was the construction of the Royal C. Johnson Veterans Hospital, which cost over $4 million dollars.[45]

Sioux Falls became a more cosmopolitan city as its citizens met young men and women from all parts of the United States. Many local homes hosted these young men and women for Sunday dinners. GIs from large urban centers who volunteered to help local farmers with harvest and haying would always remember the home-cooked and abundant food on the table in the farm home's kitchen. Social interaction included the large number of young women from southeast South Dakota who dated and married young men at the air base. After the war, several of these couples returned to live and raise their children.

The city's white population witnessed distinct segregation for the first time with the presence of many Southern white military personnel and a large contingent of African-American soldiers. The black soldiers were isolated from entertainment and business activities. They had difficulty in finding lodging and living facilities within the city. They were restricted to eating at only two restaurants, the Hamburger Inn and the Canton Café. The social limitations placed on the black GIs led to a revitalization of the NAACP in the city.

## A FINAL SALUTE

The prosperity that Sioux Falls and the nation experienced came at great cost—the young men killed or wounded in the battles that were fought on the land, sea and in the air. Many young men from the Army Technical School who sat down to Sunday dinner with city residents were later killed in action. The editor of the *Argus Leader*, on May 15, 1945, published an editorial that summed up how important the ATS and the thousands of men who learned their radio skills at the base were in the final victory over Nazi Germany:

> The doom of Germany was sealed in small part in the class rooms of Sioux Falls. In the flaming skies over Europe, these young men wrote a brilliant record. Day after day thousands of airplanes set forth from airports in England and at least half, perhaps more, carried a radio operator who had obtained his instruction in Sioux Falls. These were

the young men whom you saw in Sioux Falls, the seemingly carefree lads. Sioux Falls salutes them, all of them, salutes them for their bravery, their skill, their devotion to duty and their remarkable accomplishment. Heroes all, they are great heroes of the war that history will record in its noblest page.[46]

# NOTES

## Chapter 1

1 Reuben E. Bragstad, *Sioux Falls in Retrospect.* (Sioux Falls: privately printed, 1967), 1; Federal Writers' Project, Works Progress Administration, *A South Dakota Guide* (Pierre: South Dakota Guide Commission, 1938), 151-52.

2 R. Douglas Hurt, *The Great Plains during World War II* (Lincoln: University of Nebraska Press, 2008), 242-75.

3 Encyclopedia of American History, New York: Harper and Row, 1963, 364.

4 Karl E. Mundt Archives, Karl E. Mundt's letter to Paul K. Meyers, 6 January 1942. Karl E. Mundt Historical and Educational Foundation, Dakota State University, Madison, SD.

5 *Argus Leader*, 5 February 1942 (An editorial taken from the *Yankton Press and Dakotan*).

6 Mundt Archives, Letters from Mundt to Meyers, January 12, 13 and 16, 1942. Mundt Foundation.

7 Mundt Archives, Letter from Mundt to Claude Hamilton, 28 January 1942. Mundt Foundation.

8 *Argus Leader*, 5 February 1942.

9 Mundt Archives, Letter from Fred Christopherson to Mundt, 16 February 1942. Mundt Foundation.

10 *Argus Leader*, 27 March 1942.

11 Mundt Archives, Letter from Mundt to Henry Carlson, 19 March 1942. Mundt Foundation.

12 *Argus Leader*, 27 March 1942.

13 Ibid.; the Municipal Airport was dedicated on 15 September 1939. Bragstad, 73.

14 Ibid.

15 Ibid., 29 March 1942.

16 Ibid., 28 March 1942.

17 Ibid. 1 April 1942; 2 April 1942.

18 Ibid. Editorial, "Our Opportunity," 28 March 1942.

19 Ibid., 7 April 1942.

20 Ibid.

21 Ibid.

22 Ibid., 16 April 1942.

23 Ibid., 20 April 1942.

24 Ibid., 14 April 1942.

25 Ibid., 20 April 1942.

26 Ibid., 22 April 1942; Bragstad, 73.

27 Ibid., 31 May 1942; 4 June 1942.

28 Ibid., 4 April 1942.

29 Ibid., 8 April 1942.

30 Ibid., 4 May 1942.

31 Ibid., 11 April 1942.

32 Ibid., 20 April 1942.

33 The Corps of Engineers built a sewage plant adjacent to the city's sewage plant. The new plant had an estimated capacity of two million gallons per day. Bragstad,105.

34 *Argus Leader*, 10 April 1942.

35 Ibid., 28 April 1942.

36 Ibid., 5 April 1942.

37 Ibid., 27 March 1942.

38 Ibid., 4 April 1942.

39 Ibid., 7 April 1942.

40 Ibid., 18 April 1942.

41 Ibid., 6 April 1942.

42 Ibid., 19 May 1942.

43 Ibid., 26 April 1942

44 Ibid., 27 June 1942.

45 Ibid., 20 June 1942.

46 Ibid., 14 April 1942.

47 Ibid., 16 March 1942.

48 Ibid., 30 March 1942.

49 Ibid., 4 June 1942.

50 Ibid., 10 June 1942.

51 Ibid., 12 June 1942.

52 Ibid., 12 August 1942.

53 Ibid., 8 May 1942; 3 June 1942.

54 Ibid., 12 April 1942.

55 Ibid., 13 April 1942.

56 Ibid., 31 May 1942.

57 Ibid., 17 June 1942.

58 Ibid., 11 May 1942.

59 Ibid., 13 April 1942

60 Ibid., 12 May 1942.

61 *Polar Tech,* 22 August 1942.

62 *Argus Leader*, 26 May 1942.

63 Ibid., 31 May 1942.

64 Ibid.

65 Ibid., 7 June 1942.

66 Ibid., 1 June 1942.

67 Ibid.

68 Ibid., 14 June 1942.

69 Keith Lekness, "Soldiers in Sioux Falls? That's Right!" *Prairie People* 2:1 (1979).

70 Interview with Lil Norlin and Helge Stadem, 9 July 1984, Sioux Falls, SD.

71 *Argus Leader*, 21 July 1942.

72 Ibid., 28 June 1942

73 Marie Christopherson, *Driftwood In A Time of War* (Sioux Falls: Center for Western Studies, 1995), 15.

74 *Argus Leader*, 14 June 1942.

75 Ibid., 6 July 1942.

76 *Polar Tech*, 25 August 1944

77 "Public Address Regarding the Air Base, by Harold Hanson, 9 May 2006.

78 *Argus Leader*, 22 August 1942.

## Chapter 2

1 Impressions of J. A. Bailey, *Aberdeen American News*, cited in the *Sioux Falls Argus Leader*, 2 May 1943.

2 *Argus Leader,* 15 February 1943.

3 Interview with Charles Chamblin, a law officer in South Dakota for forty-two years. South Dakota Oral History Center, University of South Dakota (hereinafter SDOHC), Transcript #1080.

4 *Argus Leader,* 25 April 1981.

5 Ibid., 22 September 1942; 20 December 1942.

6 Ibid., 3 April 1943.

7 Ibid., 19 September 1942.

8 Ibid., 31 December 1942.

9 Ibid., 31 December 1942.

10 *Argus Leader*, 4 April 1942.

11 Ibid., 17 August 1942.

12 *Polar Tech,* 3 March 1944.

13 Ibid., 8 September 1944.

14 Ibid., 26 March 1943.

15 *Sioux Sentinel,* 21 September 1945.

16 *Argus Leader,* 4 October 1942.

17 *Polar Tech,* 13 October 1944.

18 *Argus Leader,* 20 September 1942.

19 *Polar Tech,* 25 September 1942.

20 *Sioux Sentinel,* 6 July 1945.

21 *Polar Tech,* 25 August 1944.

22 Ibid., 3 November 1944.

23 *Argus Leader,* 6 December 1942.

24 *Polar Tech,* 15 June 1945.

25 Alan Lathrop, "Designing for South Dakota and the Upper Midwest: The Career of Architect Harold T. Spitznagel, 1930-1974," *South Dakota History* 37(Winter 2007): 289.

26 *Argus Leader,* 12 September 1942. For a description of Joseph Floyd's entrepreneurial response to the ATS, the creation of *G.I. Blind Date*, see Ron Robinson's chapter, "Communications," in Harry F. Thompson, ed., *A New South Dakota History*, 2nd edition (Sioux Falls: Center for Western Studies, 2009), 470.

27 Ibid., 22 October 1942.

28 Ibid., 16 January 1966.

29 Ibid. 30 October 1942.

30 Lathrop, "Designing for South Dakota," 290.

31 *Argus Leader,* 3 May 1943.

32 Ibid., 15 June 1943; 3 September 1943.

33 *Polar Tech,* 13 November 1942.

34 *Argus Leader,* 28 March 1943; 15 June 1943.

35 Ibid., 31 August 1943.

36 Ibid., 26 December 1942.

37 *Polar Tech,* 23 June 1944.

38 Ibid., 18 February 1944.

39 Ibid., 4 February 1944.

40 Ibid., 28 April 1944.

41 Ibid., 8 January 1943.

42 Ibid., 13 September 1942.

43 *Sioux Sentinel,* 3 August 1945.

44 *Polar Tech,* 28 January 1944.

45 *Argus Leader*, 1 December 1991; *Polar Tech,* 11 December 1942.

46 Ibid., 9 November 1978.

47 Ibid., 1 January 1943; 14 February 1943.

48 Ibid., 3 September 1942.

49 Ibid., 14 February 1943.

50 Christopherson, 111.

51 *Polar Tech,* 21 July 1944.

52 *Argus Leader,* 9 November 1978.

53 Ibid., 25 August 1942.

54 Ibid., 9 November 1978.

55 Ibid., 15 November 1942.

56 Ibid., 3 August 1942.

57 Ibid. 7 January 1943.

58 Interview with Charles Chamblin, 11 July 1974, SDOHC, Transcript #1080.

59 *Argus Leader,* 21 June 1942.

60 Ibid., 21 June 1942.

61 Ibid., 13 November 1942.

62 Ibid., 13 November 1942.

63 Ibid.

64 Ibid., 10 December 1942.

65 Richard R. Lingeman, *Don't You Know There Is A War On? The American Home Front, 1941-1945* (New York: Putnam, 1980); Richard Polenberg, *War and Society: The United States, 1941-1945* (Philadelphia: J. B. Lippincott Company, 1972).

66 *Argus Leader,* 10 August 1942.

67 Ibid., 25 January 1943.

68 Ibid.

69 Ibid., 7 March 1943.

70 *Polar Tech,* 10 December 1943.

71 Ibid., 17 December 1943.

72 *Argus Leader,* 25 April 1943.

73 Ibid.

74 Ibid., 16 July 1942; 6 September 1942.

75 Ibid., 16 July 1942.

76 Ibid., 20 July 1942.

77 Ibid., 7 August 1942.

78 Ibid., 6 September 1942.

79 Ibid., 30 September 1942.

80 Ibid., 4 December 1942.

81 Ibid., 16 January1943.

82 Ibid., 11 September 1942.

83 Ibid., 2 October 1942.

84 Ibid.

85 Ibid., 29 October 1942.

86 Ibid., 21 December 1942.

87 Ibid., 17 November 1942.

88 *Polar Tech*, 6 November 1942.

89 *Argus Leader*, 11 February 1943.

90 Lathrop, "Designing for South Dakota," 290.

91 *Argus Leader*, 10 January 1943.

92 Ibid., 15 February 1943.

93 Ibid., 10 March 1943.

94 Ibid., 6 March 1943.

95 Ibid., 12 March 1993.

96 *Sioux Sentinel*, 21 September 1945.

97 Ibid., 25 September 1945.

## Chapter 3

1   Barbara W. Tuchman, *Stilwell and the American Experience in China, 1911-1945* (New York:  Macmillan Company, 1970), 203.

2   Ibid., p. 18.

3   Interview with Ted Ramsey, 13 July 1974, SDOHC, Transcript #1088.

4   *Argus Leader*, 10 July 1942.

5   *Polar Tech*, 30 October 1942.

6   Ibid., 29 January 1943.

7   Interview with Paul Graves, 13 July 1974, SDOHC, Transcript #1082.

8   Ibid.

9   Ramsey.

10 Christopherson,100.

11 Jocelyn Sue Archer, "West Troops Support the War Effort," History 140, Augustana College, Sioux Falls, South Dakota, 25 April 1978.

12 *Polar Tech*, 12 March 1943.

13 Ibid., 16 April 1943. The headquarters of the Technical Training Command said "Headquarters of the TTC considers Sioux Falls the #1 Radio School."

14 Ibid., 9 July 1943.

15 Ibid., 10 September 1943.

16 Christopherson, 303.

17 *Polar Tech*, 29 October 1943.

18 Ibid., 21 April 1944.

19 Ibid., 16 March 1945.

20 Ibid., 30 March 1945.

21 *Sioux Sentinel*, 13 July 1945.

22 Ibid., 10 August 1945.

23 *Argus Leader*, 21 July 1943.

24 *Sioux Sentinel*, 26 October 1945.

## Chapter 4

1   *Polar Tech*, 18 September 1942.

2   Graves, p.10.

3   Ibid.

4   Ramsey.

5   *Argus Leader*, 10 July 1942.

6   Ibid., 10 July 1942.

7   *Polar Tech*, 30 October 1942.

8   Ibid., 29 January 1943.

9   Graves.

10 *Polar Tech*, 6 November 1942.

11 Ibid., 25 September 1942.

12 *Polar Tech*, September 1942.

13 Arthur S. Johnson III, "A Memoir, AJS in World War II, Chapter IV, December 5, 1942-May 3, 1943."

14 Polar Tech, 21 May 1943; 4 June 1943.

15 Ibid., 16 July 1943.

16 Ibid., 16 June 1944.

17 Ibid., 23 June 1944.

18 James Gleik, *The Information: A History, A Theory, A Flood* (New York: Pantheon Books, 2011), 19-21.

19 Ibid.

20 *Polar Tech,* 11 September 1942.

21 Interview with Douglas Uthe, a Korean War veteran, 10 December 2007; Johnson.

22 *Polar Tech,* September 1942.

23 Ibid., 9 September 1943.

24 Ibid., 25 February 1944; 28 July 1944.

25 Ibid., 13 November 1942.

26 Ibid., 14 January 1944; 17 March 1944.

27 Ibid., 20 October 1944.

28 Graves.

29 *Polar Tech,* 1 October 1943.

30 Ibid., 23 July 1943.

31 Ibid., 6 August 1943.

32 Ibid., 23 July 1943.

33 Ibid., 12 May 1944.

34 Ibid., 6 August 1943; *Argus Leader,* 1 August 1943.

35 Ibid., 11 August 1944.

36 Ibid., 1 December 1944; 5 January 1945.

37 Ibid., 1 June 1945.

38 Ibid., 20 November 1942

39 Ibid., 11 December 1943.

40 Ibid., 17 September 1943.

41 Ibid., 22 January 1943.

42 Ibid., 26 September 1943.

43 Ibid., 19 September 1943.

44 Ibid., 18 August 1944.

45 Ibid., 28 July 1944.

46 Ibid., 20 August 1943.

47 Ibid., 23 March 1945.

48 Ibid., 9 March 1945.

49 Johnson.

50 Ibid.

51 Ibid.

52 Ibid.

53 *Polar Tech*, 27 April 1945.

54 Ibid., 30 March 1945; 14 May 1945; 25 May 1945.

## Chapter 5

1  *Polar Tech,* June 1943.

2  *Argus Leader,* 23 June 1943.

3  *Polar Tech,* 21 May 1943; *Argus Leader,* 16 May 1943.

4  *Argus Leader,* 16 May 1943; 23 June 1943.

5  Ibid., 3 August 1943.

6  *Polar Tech,* 30 July 1943.

7  *Argus Leader,* 15 August 1943.

8  *Polar Tech,* 13 August 1943; *Argus Leader,* 15 August 1943.

9  Ibid., 29 August 1943; *Argus Leader,* 12 September 1943.

10 *Polar Tech,* 15 October 1943.

11 Ibid., 9 June 1944.

12 Ibid., 9 July 1943.

13 Ibid., 21 April 1944.

14 *Argus Leader,* 20 June 1943.

15 Public Notice. Request for information about the former Sioux Falls Army Air Field Rifle Range, U.S. Army Corps of Engineers, Omaha District.  Between March 29 and May 18 1946, leases on the rifle range were terminated and the property was returned to the original owners.

16 *Polar Tech,* 25 June 1943.

17 Ibid., 27 October 1944.

18 Ibid., 6 October 1944.

19 Ibid, 17 November 1944.

20 Ibid., 19 November 1944.

21 Ibid.

22 Ibid., 24 December 1943.

23 Ibid., 22 August 1943; 15 January 1943.

24 Ibid., 16 July 1943.

25 Hurt, 202.

26 Ibid.

27 Ibid.

28 *Sioux Sentinel,* 17 July 1945.

29 *Argus Leader,* 18 July 1943.

30 *Polar Tech,* 23 July 1943.

31 *Argus Leader,* 10 August 1943.

32 *Polar Tech,* 14 July 1944.

33 *Sioux Sentinel,* 3 August 1945.

## Chapter 6

1 Johnson.

2 Graves.

3 *Polar Tech*, 21 August 1942.

4 *Radiomen: The Story of the Sioux Falls Army Air Forces Technical Command Radio Training School,* Sioux Falls: Siouxland Heritage Museums, 2000.

5 Johnson

6 Francis Mainolfi, quoted in the *Argus Leader,* 9 November 1978.

7 *Polar Tech,* 18 February 1944.

8 Ibid., 16 February 1945.

9 Graves.

10 Mainolfi.

11 *Polar Tech,* 18 February 1944.

12 Ibid.

13 Ibid.

14 Ibid., 25 February 1944.

15 Christopherson, 268.

16 *Radiomen*.

17 Ibid.

18 Johnson.

19 *Polar Tech,* 1 December 1944.

20 Ibid., 24 March 1944.

21 Ibid., 6 October 1944.

22 Ibid., 12 January 1945.

23 Christopherson, 268.

24 *Polar Tech,* 15 January 1945.

25 Ibid., 22 December 1944.

26 Ibid., 12 November 1943.

27 *Argus Leader,* 9 November 1978.

28 *Polar Tech,* 12 January 1945.

29 Graves.

30 *Polar Tech,* 30 March 1945.

31 Ibid., 6 April 1945.

32 Ibid., 18 May 1945.

33 Ibid., 13 April 1945.

34 Ibid., 8 June 1945.

35 *Argus Leader,* 30 March 1943.

36 Ibid., 14 May 1943.

37 *Polar Tech,* June 9 1945.

38 *Argus Leader,* 1 December 1991.

39 *Radiomen*.

40 Johnson. In a recent comment Johnson said, "I certainly was not living in hardship. People were nice."

41 *Argus Leader,* 13 July 1942.

42 *Polar Tech,* 21 July 1944.

43 Ibid., 28 April 1944.

44 *Polar Tech,* 28 April 1944; 30 June 1944.

45 Ibid., 11 August 1944.

46 Graves.

47 *Polar Tech,* 11 August 1944; 15 December 1944.

48 *Argus Leader,* 9 December 1984.

49 Ibid., 29 March 2001.

50 Ibid., 19 January 1945.

51 Ibid., 5 January 1945.

## Chapter 7

1 As noted earlier, the base could not be named George Field as

proposed by Colonel Camblin. Sioux Falls *Argus Leader,* 21 July 1942.

2 *Argus Leader,* 4 October 1942.

3 Graves.

4 *Polar Tech,* 30 October 1942.

5 Ibid., 6 November 1942.

6 *Argus Leader,* 25 May 1992.

7 Ibid., 17 January 1943, excerpted from *Polar Tech.*

8 Ibid.

9 Bragstad.

10 Ibid.

11 Interview with Maurice Coakley, 16 July 1976, SDOHC, Transcript #1109.

12 Coakley indicated that when they went to a movie they had no problem choosing where they wanted to sit.

13 Coakley.

14 Graves.

15 *Argus Leader,* 29 November 1942.

16 Ibid.

17 Coakley. The new facility was in the Brooks Building. In 1975, the Federal Credit Union occupied the building.

18 Ibid.

19 *Argus Leader,* 8 March 1943.

20 *Polar Tech,* 28 April 1944.

21 Graves.

22 *Polar Tech,* 24 December 1943.

23 Ibid., 5 February 1943.

24 Ibid., 7 January 1944.

25 Ibid., 15 January 1943.

26 *Sioux Sentinel,* 19 October 1945.

27 *Polar Tech,* 16 April 1943.

28 Ibid., 17 March 1944.

29 Graves.

30 *Argus Leader,* 30 September 1943.

31 Ibid., Chamber of Commerce insert, 1992. See also Phil Dixon, *The Negro Baseball Leagues: A Photographic History* (Mattituck, NY: Amereon, 1992); *Sioux Sentinel,* 31 August 1945.

32 *Polar Tech*, August 1945.

33 *Argus Leader*, Chamber of Commerce insert, 1992.

34 *Sioux Sentinel,* 20 July 1945.

35 *Polar Tech,* 3 March 1944.

36 "Yuletide Cheer Flies South as ATS Negroes Aid Kiddies," *Argus Leader*, 20 December 1942.

37 *Argus Leader* editorial "Off the Beam," 23 December 1942; *Business Week*, 12 December 1942.

38 Ibid.

39 Interview with Bessie Vaughn, 29 August 1974, SDOHC, Tape #1195.

40 Graves.

41 Prentiss L. Pemberton, "Our Negro Policy," *Argus Leader*, 13 February 1943.

42 Army Air Forces Technical School, Sioux Falls, South Dakota, Class Twenty-Four. n.d.

43 Steve Young, "Fighting Two Battles," *Argus Leader,* 25 May 1992.

## Chapter 8

1 1 *Polar Tech,* 18 September 1942.

2 *Argus Leader,* 23 July 1942.

3 Ibid., 21 July 1942.

4 Ibid., 8 August 1942.

5 Christopherson,108.

6 *Radiomen*, 8.

7 Ibid., p. 12.

8 *Polar Tech,* 8 January 1943.

9 *Radiomen*, 10.

10 *Polar Tech,* 3 November 1942.

11 Ibid., 8 January 1943; 23 April 1943.

12 Graves.

13 Debra O'Connor, "Sioux Falls: Nicest Army Town Any GI Ever Hit," *Argus Leader,* 9 November 1978;

*Argus Leader,* 14 April 2000.

14 *Polar Tech,* 21 July 1944.

15 Newsletter, Station Hospital, Vol. 1, No.1, 17 June 1943. File 1, AB/10, Sioux Falls Air Base Collection, Center for Western Studies (hereinafter CWS), Augustana College, Sioux Falls, SD.

16 *Argus Leader,* 29 August 1943.

17 File 3F, 1/1, AB /10, Air Base Collection, CWS; *Polar Tech,* 5 February 1943.

18 Christopherson, 251.

19 1/1, File AB/11, Air Base Collection, CWS.

20 Christopherson, 150.

21 *Polar Tech,* 16 October 1942.

22 *Argus Leader,* 20 September 1942.

23 *Polar Tech,* 13 September 1942; 25 August 1944.

24 Ibid., 8 December 1944.

25 Ibid., 10 September 1943.

26 Ibid., 2 February 1945.

27 *Sioux Sentinel,* 30 November 1945.

28 Ramsey.

29 *Polar Tech,* 19 March 1943.

30 Ibid., 11 June 1943.

31 Ibid., 25 June 1943.

32 Ibid., 9 July 1943.

33 Ibid., 3 September 1943.

34 Ibid., 13 August 1943.

35 *Sioux Sentinel,* 10 August 1945.

36 Ibid., 9 June 1944.

37 *Sioux Sentinel,* 31 August 1945.

38 Ibid., 17 August 1945.

## Chapter 9

1 *Polar Tech,* 1 November 1942.

2 *Argus Leader*, 14 September 1942.

3 Ibid., 7 July 1942; interview with Charles Chamblin, 11 July 1974 SDOHC, Transcript #1080.

4 Ibid., 1 January 1943.

5 Ibid., 3 January 1943.

6 Ibid.

7 Chamblin.

8 Graves.

9 *Argus Leader*, 9 January 1943.

10 *Argus Leader*, 21 November 1942; 14 March 1943.

11 Police Reports, *Argus Leader*, 1942-1944.

12 Ibid.

13 *Argus Leader,* 16 May 1943.

14 Ibid., 1 August 1942.

15 *Polar Tech,* 27 August 1943.

16 *Argus Leader,* 20 November 1942.

17 *Polar Tech,* 5 March 1943.

18 Graves.

19 *Argus Leader,* 26 September 1943.

20 Ibid., 14 May 1943.

21 Ibid., 31 May 1943.

22 Ibid., 23 June 1943.

23 Ibid., 26 January 1943; 5 February 1943.

24 Ibid., 31 December 1975; 4 October 1943.

## Chapter 10

1 *Polar Tech,* October 1942.

2 Ibid., 19 November 1943.

3 Howard Hanson, Sioux Falls resident, 9 May 2006.

4 Lekness; *Argus Leader,* 1 September 1942.

5 Hanson, 9 May 2006.

6 *Polar Tech,* 26 February 1943.

7 Ibid., 19 February 1943.

8 Ibid., 31 March 1944.

9 Ibid., 19 February 1943.

10 Ibid., 25 September 1942.

11 Christopherson, 268.

12 *Argus Leader*, 20 June 1943.

13 *Polar Tech,* 19 February 1943.

14 Christopherson, 25.

15 Ibid., 26 February 1943.

16 Ibid., June 1944.

17 Ibid., 25 April 1943.

18 Ibid., 7 April 1944.

19 Ibid., 19 September 1942.

20 Ibid.

21 Ibid., 26 May 1944.

22 Ibid., 22 September 1944.

23 Ibid., 4 August 1944.

24 *Polar Tech,* 20 July 1943.

25 Ibid., 22 June 1945.

26 Ibid., 1 October 1943.

27 Ibid., 12 September 1943.

28 Ibid., 21 October 1943.

29 Ibid., 8 August 1943.

30 Ibid., 10 April 1943.

31 Ibid., 2 June 1944.

32 *Sioux Sentinel,* 6 July 1945.

33 *Polar Tech,* 25 September 1942.

34 Ibid., 21 May 1943.

35 Ibid., 28 October 1943.

36 Ibid., 29 September 1944.

37 Ibid., 3 March 1944.

38 Ibid., 6 June 1943.

39 Ibid., 9 April 1943.

40 Ibid., 6 June 1943.

41 Ibid., 9 April 1943; Christopherson, 132.

42 *Polar Tech,* 31 December 1943.

43 Ibid., 7 May 1943.

44 *Sioux Sentinel,* 13 July 1945.

45 Ibid., 12 March 1943.

46 Ibid., 12 March 1943.

47 Ibid., 23 April 1943.

48 *Argus Leader,* 14 July 1943.

49 Ibid., 25 January 1943.

50 *Sioux Sentinel,* 9 November 1945; *Polar Tech,* 2 April 1943.

51 *Argus Leader,* 30 May 1943.

52 *Polar Tech,* 20 November 1942.

53 *Argus Leader,* 15 May 1943.

54 Ibid., 6 June 1943.

55 *Polar Tech*, 3 September 1943.

56 Ibid., 26 September 1943.

57 Ibid., 31 March 1944.

58 Ibid., 16 July 1943.

59 Christopherson, 63-64.

60 *Polar Tech,* 28 June 1944.

61 Ibid., 28 January 1944.

62 Ibid., 5 March 1943.

63 Ibid., 24 March 1944.

64 Ibid., 5 February 1943.

65 Ibid., August 1942.

66 Ibid., March 1943.

67 *Sioux Sentinel,* 20 July 1945.

68 *Argus Leader,* 30 June 1942; 30 May 1943; *Polar Tech,* 28 May 1943.

## Chapter 11

1 *Argus Leader,* 25 June 1942.

2 Hurt, 242-45, 402.

3 *Sioux Falls City Directory* (Omaha: R. L. Polk and Co., 1942), XLV.

4   Pearl S. Anderson, "Life in Sioux Falls during World War II," History 140, Augustana College, 1965.

5   Anderson; Helen Gottsleben, in Charles Woodard, ed., *On the Homefront: South Dakota Stories* (Brookings: South Dakota Humanities Council, 2007), 20.

6   Norlin and Stadem.

7   Christopherson, 108; Woodard, 19-20.

8   Anderson; Woodard, 20.

9   *Argus Leader,* 25 April 1981.

10 Ibid.

11 Ibid., 1 December 1991.

12 Archer.

13 Norlin and Stadem.

14 Christopherson, 109.

15 Betty Nagel, in Woodard, 19.

16 Anderson.

17 Woodard, 21.

18 Archer.

19 *Argus Leader*, 24 January 1943.

20 Ibid., 3 January 1943.

21 *Sioux Falls City Directory*, 1942, XLV.

22 Mary Jarratt, "The Big Bands," History 165, Augustana College, 21 January 1980.

23 Ibid.

24 Ibid.

25 Selwyn Farrington, Jr., *Railroads at War* (New York: Coward-McCann, 1944).

26 Archer.

27 Ibid.

## Chapter 12

1   John Keegan, *The Second World War (*New York, Penguin Books, 1990), 430-33.

2   *Polar Tech,* 11 May 1945.

3   *Polar Tech,* 16 March 1945.

4   Ibid., 30 March 1945.

5   Ibid., 27 April 1945.

6   Ibid., 13 April 1945.

7   Ibid., 30 March 1945.

8   Ibid., 18 May 1945.

9   Ibid., 25 May 1945.

10 *Sioux Sentinel,* 29 June 1945.

11 "Bomber Rams Skyscraper," Historical Marker Dedication Program" (Sioux Falls: Minnehaha County Historical Society), 29 March 2001. The marker is located at the north side of West Algonquin St., Sioux Falls, SD.

12 *Sioux Sentinel*, 7 September 1945.

13 *Argus Leader,* 16 January 1966; Alan K. Lathrop, "Army Field Closed 20 Years Ago," History 140, Augustana College, n.d.

14 Jerry W. Whiting and Wayne B. Whiting, *I'm Off to War, Mother, But I'll Be Back: Reflections of a World War II Tail Gunner* (Walnut Creek, CA: Tarnaby Books, 2001), 208-09.

15 *Sioux Sentinel,* 17 August 1945.

16 Ramsey.

17 Whiting and Whiting.

18 Graves.

19 Ramsey.

20 *Argus Leader,* 13 August 1950.

21 *Sioux Sentinel*, 14 September 1945.

22 Ibid., 7 September 1945.

23 *Polar Tech,* 11 May 1945.

24 *Sioux Sentinel,* 28 September 1945.

25 Ibid.

26 Ibid., 6 July 1945.

27 Ibid., 21 September 1945.

28 Ibid., 16 November 1945.

29 Ibid.

30 Ibid., 21 September 1945.

31 Ibid., 26 October 1945.

32 Ibid., 17 November 1945.

33 *Sioux Sentinel,* 2 November 1945.

34 *Argus Leader,* 30 December 1945.

35 Ibid., 9 November 1945; 30 November 1945.

36 Archer; Lathrop, "Army Field Closed 20 Years Ago."

37 *Argus Leader,* 30 December 1945.

38 Sioux Falls Air Base Collection, CWS, 1/1AB 12.

39 *Argus Leader,* 19 April 1948.

40 Ibid., 18 February 1948; 14 July 1948.

41 Ibid., 27 August 1948.

42 Donald E. Brown, *When We Were Young: Childhood: A Santa Barbara Anthology*, Grace Rachow, ed. (Santa Barbara, CA: A Community of Voices, 2000).

43 *Argus Leader*, 9 July 1947.

44 Interview with Judee Koplow Epstein, 29 September 1976, SDOHC, Tape #1111.

45 *Argus Leader*, 13 August 1950.

46 Ibid., 15 May 1945.

# WORKS CITED

## Published Works

"Bomber Rams Skyscraper." Historical Marker Dedication Program. Sioux Falls: Minnehaha County Historical Society. 29 March 2001.

Bragstad, Reuben. *Sioux Falls in Retrospect.* Sioux Falls: privately printed, 1967.

Brown, Donald E. *When We Were Young: Childhood: A Santa Barbara Anthology.* Edited by Grace Rachow. Santa Barbara, CA: A Community of Voices, 2000.

Christopherson, Marie. *Driftwood In a Time of War.* Sioux Falls: Center for Western Studies, 1995.

Dixon, Phil. *The Negro Baseball Leagues: A Photographic History.* Mattituck, NY: Amereon, 1992.

*Encyclopedia of American History.* New York: Harper & Row, 1962.

Farrington, Selwyn. *Railroads at War.* New York: Coward-McCann, 1944.

Federal Writers' Project, Works Progress Administration, comp. *A South Dakota Guide.* Pierre: South Dakota Guide Commission, 1938.

Futrell, Frank. "The Development of Base Facilities." *The Army Air Forces in World War II.* Vol. 6. Edited by Wesley F. Craven and James L. Cate. Chicago: University of Chicago Press, 1955.

Gleik, James. *The Information: A History, a Theory, a Flood.* New York: Pantheon Books, 2011.

Hurt, R. Douglas. *The Great Plains during World War II.* Lincoln: University of Nebraska Press, 2008.

Keegan, John. *The Second World War*. New York: Penguin Books, 1990.

Lathrop, Alan. K. "Designing for South Dakota and the Upper Midwest: The Career of Architect Harold T. Spitznagel, 1930-1974." *South Dakota History* 37 (Winter 2007): 271–305.

Lekness, Keith. "Soldiers in Sioux Falls? That's Right!" *Prairie People* 2:1 (1979): 3-7.

Lingeman, Richard R. *Don't You Know There's a War On? The American Home Front, 1941-1945*. New York: Putnam, 1980.

Polenberg, Richard. *War and Society: The United States, 1941-1945*. Philadelphia: J. B. Lippincott Company, 1972.

*Radiomen: The Story of the Sioux Falls Army Air Forces Technical Command Radio Training School*. Sioux Falls: Siouxland Heritage Museums, 2000.

Thompson, Harry F., ed. *A New South Dakota History*, 2nd ed. Sioux Falls: Center for Western Studies, 2009.

Tuchman, Barbara. *Stilwell and the American Experience in China, 1911-1945*. New York: Macmillan Company, 1970.

Whiting, Jerry W. and Wayne B. Whiting. *I'm Off To War, Mother, But I'll Be Back: Reflections of a World War II Tail Gunner.* Walnut Creek, CA: Tarnaby Books, 2001.

Woodard, Charles L., ed. *On the Homefront: South Dakota Stories.* Brookings: South Dakota Humanities Council, 2007.

## Archival Sources
### The Center for Western Studies, Augustana College, Sioux Falls, South Dakota

Army Air Forces Technical School newspaper clippings.

Class Annual from the Army Air Forces Technical School, Sioux Falls, SD.

Newsletters from the Station Hospital. Sioux Falls Army Technical School, Sioux Falls, SD.

*Polar Tech*. Weekly newspaper of the Army Technical School, 1942-1945.

*Sioux Sentinel*. Weekly newspaper of the Army Technical School, 1945.

## The South Dakota Oral History Center, University of South Dakota, Vermillion, South Dakota

Chamblin, Charles. Interview. 11 July 1974. Transcript #1080.

Coakley, Maurice. Interview. 16 July 1976. Transcript #1109.

Epstein, Judee Koplow. Interview. 29 September 1976. Tape #1111.

Gowan, Alfred M. Interview. 6 August 1971. Tape #269.

Graves, Paul and Mary. Interview. 13 July 1974. Transcript #1082.

Harvey, Edgar. Interview. 27 June 1974. Tape #1072.

Lee, Georgia. Interview. 28 August 1974. Tape #1185.

Ramsey, Ted. Interview. 13 July 1974. Transcript #1088.

Vaughn, Bessie. Interview. 29 August 1974. Tape #1195.

## Other

Anderson, Pearl. "Life in Sioux Falls during World War II." History 140. Augustana College, 1965.

Archer, Jocylen Sue. "West Troops Support the War Effort." History 140. Augustana College, 1978.

Army Air Forces Technical School Syllabus (training content for each week in a 20-week course).

Hanson, Harold. "Public Address Regarding the Air Base." Sioux Falls: 9 May 2006.

Hanson, Howard. Interview by Lynwood E. Oyos. 9 May 2006. Sioux Falls, SD.

Jarratt, Mary. "The Big Bands." History 165. Augustana College, 21 July 1980.

Johnson, Arthur S. III. "A Memoir, AJS in World War II: Daily Journal at the Army Technical School, 1942-1943."

Lathrop, Alan K. "Army Field Closed 20 Years Ago," History 140, Augustana College, 16 January 1966.

Lorenz, Al. Interview by Lynwood E. Oyos. November 2009. Sioux Falls, SD.

Mundt, Karl E. Mundt Archives. Mundt Historical and Educational Foundation. Madison, SD.

Norlin, Lil and Helge Stadem. Interview by Lynwood E. Oyos. 9 July 1984. Sioux Falls, SD.

Northwestern Bell Telephone Company. "Handbook of Information on Sioux Falls." Given to Newcomers to the Technical School, nd.

Petry, Howard J. and Oscar L. Rogers. "History of the Flight Line Sioux Falls Army Airfield, Sioux Falls, South Dakota, July 1942-March 1944."

*Sioux Falls Argus Leader*. 1942-1945, 1966, 1978, 1981, 1984, 1992, 2000, 2001.

"Soldiers in Civies." A Manual of Information for Civilian Employees.

Uthe, Douglas. Interview by Lynwood E. Oyos, 10 December 2007. Sioux Falls, SD.

# INDEX

## A

Adams, Rev. Clarence W., 13

African Americans, 90, 111-24, 132-33

agriculture, 1, 90-93

aircraft identification, 160

Algona, IA, 190

Allen, Jay B., 8

Amarillo, TX, ix

American Legion, 3

Anderson, Pearl S., vi

anti-aircraft guns, 85, 180

Archer, Jocelyn, vi

Arkota Ball Room, 1, 27, 154, 176

Armstrong, Jack, 112, 123-24

Armstrong, Louis, 154, 176

Army Air Corps/Forces Technical Training Command, viii, 23-24

Army Air Forces band, 153; hospital, 130

Arnold, Gen. Henry "Hap," viii

assaults on women, 141-42

AT-12 aircraft, 84-85

AT-18 collision (Dec. 8, 1944), 107-10

Augustana College, 117, 191-92

Augustana Lutheran Church, 30, 33

Austin, C.M., 24

Australia, 10, 81

Autry, Gene, 155

AWOL, 140, 163

## B

B-17 Flying Fortress bombers, 63, 66, 71-72, 74, 125, 180-83

B-24 Liberator bombers, 63, 72, 74, 125

B-25 Billy Mitchell bombers, 72, 85, 106

Bailey, J. A., 26

bank clearings, 28-29

barrack life, 94-103

barrack stoves, 95-98

baseball, 118-23

basic training, 86-87

Bataan, 10

Berdahl, Anna, 23

Berdahl, James, 5

"big bands," 154-55, 176-77

Big Sioux River, ix, x, 12 18, 21, 37, 190

black marketeers, 140

Blair, Capt. Donald, 10

Blakey, Col. George A., 59

Blegen, N.I., 41

blinker code, 75-76

bootlegger, 139

Borgen Chevrolet, 33

Boy Scout survey, 15

Boyce, L. F., 3

Bragstad, Reuben, 3-4

Braithwaite, Gail, 5

Brandt Engineering Co., 11

breadboards, 64–65

broadcast facilities, 152-53

Brown, Knapp, x

Bruce, SD, 73

"bubble stations," 63

Bulow, William J., 4

Burns, Roy, 4, 6

## C

Cactus Heights, 87

calisthenics, 135

calories, 147

Camblin, Col. Roy W., 10, 14, 23-24, 49

camouflage, 87

canning, 173

Cannan, Edith, 126

Carlson, Henry, 4

Carlson, Jim, vii

Carpenter Hotel, 13

Case, Francis, 3

Cataract Hotel, 142

Catholic services, 34, 36, 160, 191

celebration (VJ-Day), 132, 185-87

censorship, 152

Center for Western Studies, vi, vii, 207-08

"charity girls," 40

Chase, Fred, 2

chemical warfare, 160

Cheney, Lt. Naomi Cathleen (murder), 142-44

Chicago, Milwaukee & St. Paul, 24, 177-78

Chocolate Shop, 35, 38,175

Christopherson, C.A., 5

Christopherson, Fred, 4

Christopherson, Marie, vi, 23, 36

churches (see under congregations and faiths)

civilian jobs, 191-92

class schedule, 63

"classroom in the air," 72-73

Coakley, Maurice, 114

coal and dust pneumonia, 98

Columbus College, 33, 160

Columbus Normal School, 125

communication, 151-53

construction, 15-25

contagious disease, 24

control tower, 89

Conway, Judge Walter, 137

Cook, Don, 6

Corps Army Engineers, 12

Cote, Col. Narcisse L., 24, 49-53, 63, 76, 84, 91, 103-04, 115, 125, 132-33, 140

court-martial, 141

Covert Training Unit, 84-86

Covert, Sgt. Howard L., 84

crash crew, 88-89

Crill, Louis N., 43-44

crime, 137-44

Cromwell, Lt. Jean, 133

Cubs (aircraft), 73

Culey, Aaron, vii

## D

dancing (USO), 31-37

Davis, Chester (WFA), 90

day rooms, 155

dental clinic, 160

detention center, 40

dieticians, 147

direction finding, 67, 69, 77

discharge center, 187-90

discipline problems, 160-64

dit-dahs, 69-70

Dorsey, Tommy, 176

Douglas C-47, 75

draft, 49

draw down (redeployment), 180-94

dressing for the cold, 102

*Driftwood in a Time of War*, 36

Raymond, Dana, 6

## E

East Side Lutheran Church, 33, 174

Egyptian Theater, 27

Eighth Air Force, 180

Eighty-Fifth Aviation Squadron, 112

Eisenhower, Gen. Dwight, 182

Eitreim, Louis M., 166

Elbe River, 182

electrical fundamentals, 64-68

Elmwood Golf Course, 87

Emergency Price Control Act, 168

Empire State Building collision (1945), 184

English Channel, 85

entertainment, 153-59, 174-77

Epstein, Sgt. Sidney, 128-29

Erickson, Dr. Emil, 37

## F

farm laborers, 90-93

farm women, 171

fatalities, 107-10

Federal Housing Administration, 41

Federal Security Agency, 34

Fickel, Gen. Jacob, 87

Field, George, 10

First Reformed Church, 191

First Lutheran Church, 13, 33, 174

First Methodist Church, 118

Floyd, Joseph (Joe), 8, 33

food, 147-51, 175-76

Foote, Col. Philippe, 59

Forslund, Carl N., 45

Furniture Mart Building, 13-14

## G

Galvin, J.W., 27, 137-38

Galvin, Vincent, 32

Garber, Jan, 176

gasoline rationing, 170-71

General Classification Test, 63

George, Gen. Harold, 10

German POWs, 190

German submarines, 169

"Gestapo Unit," 77

Getty Abstract Company, 6

"Gigstapo Unit," 160

GI rent complaints, 46-47

Glee Club, 118, 154

Goldsboro, NC, ix

Goodman, Benny, 176

Goodrich, Mrs. E. B., 31, 153

Grand Island, NE, 4

Graves, Mary, 127-128, 186

Graves, Sgt. Paul, vi, 51, 122, 127

"graveyard" shift, 64

Gray Lady Corps, 130-31

Great Depression, 1-2

Green Gables Cabin Camp, 139

Greensboro, NC, ix

Grimes, Mrs. W.E., 130

grocery prices, 167-68

Groups Per Minute, 70-72

Gulfport, MS, ix

Gurney, Sen. Chan, 4, 7, 24

## H

Hamilton, Claude, 3

Hansen, Mag, 176

Harley, Cpl. Walter R., 117

Harris, William, 123

harvest volunteers, 90-93

healthcare, 159-60

"help" sessions, 82

Henderson, Leon, 14

Hervig, Betty, 125

Hetherington, Lt. Col. Travis, 15

Hickson, Sgt. Reuben J., 118

Highway 16, 138

Hildreth, Johnnie, 113

Hillgren, Ralph O., 13

Hines, Gen. Frank T., 160

Hirsh, Lt. Joseph, 38, 40

holiday observances, 153, 157

Hollywood Theater, 27

hosting mothers, 157

house on 31st Street, 116-17

housing, 14-15, 41-48

Hummel, Marjorie, 125

Huron, SD, 3

Hurt, R. Douglas, vi, 2

Hurwitz, Louis, 34

## I

incoming procedures, 189

industrial park, 191

in-flight training, 71

intoxication, 138-39

inspections and uniforms, 160

instruction, 61-83

Instructor Training Division, 61

Isakson, A.A., 8

Iverson, Sherman, 30

## J

Japanese, 174

Jarratt, Dr. Mary, vi

jazz, 176

Jefferson Barracks, MO, 24

Jewish services, 33, 35, 128

John Morrell Co., 11, 28, 142

Johnson, Arthur S., III, vi, 79-82, 94-96, 98-99, 105

Johnsrud, Lois, 127

journalists, 149-50

## K

Kane, Col. John R., 58

Kansas City, MO, 135

Kearns, UT, ix

Keegan, John, vii

Keith, Walter, 137

Kemp, David, vii

Kennedy, M.A., 28

Khaki Pals, 31, 153

Kitchen Patrol, 90

Kiwanis, 38

Koethe, Romeo E., 142

Koplow (Epstein), Judee, ix, 128-29, 192

Krueger, Zelda, 130

## L

labor relations, 20

Lacy property, 87

Lafayette, MN, 73

Lake Preston, SD, 142

"latch-key" children, 136

Lathrop, Alan, vii

laundry, 146-47

Leavenworth, KS, 140

Leber, Vincent, 92

Lee, Sgt. Horace J., 112

life off-base, 145-66

Lincoln County, 14

Lincoln, Maj. Gen. Rush B., 3

Lincoln, NE, ix

Link Trainers, 72-74

liquor sales, 138

living quarters, 94-98

Lockheed Hudson bombers (AT-18s), 73, 75

Long Beach, CA, 81

Lowry Field, 10

## M

MacArthur, Gen. Douglas, 82

Madison, WI, ix, 82

Mainolfi, Francis, 36, 97

Mallory, Col. Louie, 56-57

marching band, 153

Margulies, Benjamin, 116

marriages, 130

Marshall, Gen. George C., 49

Martin, Gen. Frederick, 24

May, Robert, 6

M'Cauley, Cpl. LeRoy, 117

McKee, Mayor John, 3, 6, 11-12

McNutt, Paul V. (WMC), 90

mess halls, 147-50

Meyers, Paul K., 2-4, 12-13

mid-air collision (AT-18), 107-10

Mid-Continent Airline, x, 16

Midland Radio and Television School, 135

Mikkelsen Library Media Services (Augustana), vii

Military Police (MPs), 24, 88, 90, 138, 162

Missouri River, 3

mock fuselages, 72, 85

model advanced air base, 84

Monroe, Vaughn, 176

Morse code, 68

Mortrude, Melvin, 13

motion pictures, 175

Mundt, Karl E., vi, 2-5, 7

Mundt Historical and Educational Fdn., Karl, vi

Mundt, Mrs. Henry, 130

music, 153-55, 176

# N

National Association of Air Force Women, 132

National Defense Appropriation Act, 2

National Personnel Records Center (NPRC), vi

Nazi Germany, 82

Nedey, Val Rae (Hill), 142

Nelson, Amy, vii

Nelson, Joseph, 11

Nichols, Lt. Joseph, 190

nickelodeon, 175

Nord, Evans, 8

Norlin (Kleinsasser), Lil, 18, 21, 22, 172

Norlin and Stadem's Acme Concrete Co., 18, 21-22

Norris, Sen. George, 4

# O

Office of Price Administration (OPA), 14, 168

Office of War Information (OWI), 138

Ohm's Law, 61, 66

"Old John Feather Merchant," 184

Olsen, Stanley, 13

Omaha, NE, 74

Oral History Center, University of South Dakota, vi, 208

Orpheum Theater, 175

Orvedahl, Mrs. Francis N., 142

Ostlund, Herman, 143

Our Savior's Lutheran Church, 191

Owens, Jesse, 120-21, 155

# P

Pacific Theater, 183

Paige, Satchel, 119-20

Palace of Sweets, 35, 38, 175

Parker, SD, 92

Pass System, 164-65

passenger plane service, 11

patriotism, 173-74

Patton, Gen. George M., 182

peacetime army, 49

Pearl Harbor, viii

Pemberton, Prentiss, 122

Permanent Party, vi, 88

Perryman, W.L., 165

"Personality Girls," 131

pheasant hunting, 31

Philippine Islands, 50

Phillips Avenue, 24

physical training, 87

Pick, Lewis A., 10

pigeons, 86

Pilgrim Baptist Church, 114

point system, 187-88

*Polar Tech*, vi

popular food items, 148

post exchange, 145-46

Powsner, Lewis W., 67

prosperity, new, 27-29

prostitution, 38-41, 165

Pruitt, Gene, 6

punishments, 140

# Q

Quartermaster General, 147

Quartermaster Marketing Center, 147

# R

racial prejudice, 111-24, 132-33

Radio Dictionary, 67-68

radio instruction, 61-83

radio operator-mechanic (ROM), 64, 79-83, 107, 183-84

Raiders, 119-20, 158

railroads, 151, 177-79

Ramsey, Ted, 51, 187

Rapid City, SD, vii, 16

ration stamp points, 168-69

rationing, 167-172

Readjustment Act, 188

Reeves, Col. Raymond, 183

recreation, 13, 31-37

Red Cross Gray Ladies, 130

redeployment center, 183-84

Rediwill, Dr. F. H., 40

Regensburg, Germany, 181

rehab work, 159

Reid, Pvt. Algie, 117

rent gouging, 43

rents, 14

reorganization, 55

restaurants, 175-76

Roberts, Ralph, 8

Robinson, Col. F.H., 53-54

Rogers, Col. Oscar L., 53-56, 108, 153, 183

Rogers, Mrs. O. L., 132

Rohlffs, C. D., 13, 42

Roosevelt, Franklin D., 2, 170

Roseland Club, 114

"Rosie the Riveters," 135

Rotary, 38, 40

Royal C. Johnson Veterans Hospital, 160

rubber, 170-71

Rufer, C.J., 15-16

rug making, 131

runways, x

Russian Army, 182

Rysdon, Max, 3

# S

Sadie Hawkins, 32

Salem, SD, 93

Schweinfurt, Germany, 181

Scott Field, IL, 23, 61

Scribner, Sgt. Edward M., 152

Seargant Buck (dog), 161

Searls, Fred J., 137-38

Second Air Force, 152, 184

security units, 88-90

segregation, 114-16, 122, 124

Separation Center, 188

sexual assault, 142-44

Shannon, Capt. J.E., 112-14, 118, 132, 163

Sharpe, Gov. M. Q., 53, 153

"shooting a bearing," 67

Sinatra, Frank, 176

Sioux Chevrolet Company, 10

Sioux City, IA, 116

Sioux Falls Chamber of Commerce, 2-3, 5, 7, 10, 12-13, 29-30, 41, 43

Sioux Falls Construction Co., 18

Sioux Falls bond issue, 7-10; building boom, 190-93; defense council, 13; economic growth, 191-93; fire department, 165-66; hospitality,12-14, 29-31; library, 156, 174; police department, 139-44; radio stations, 153

Sioux Falls Ministerial Association, 13

*Sioux Sentinel*, 152

Sioux Steel Company, 28

Sioux Syndicate Company, 146

Sioux Valley Camp, 131

Siouxland Heritage Museums, vii

Smith, David H., 8

smoke and coal dust, 105

Soo Skyways, x

Soria, Pvt. Manuel, 141

South Dakota State Employment Service, 17

Spitznagel, Harold, vii, 44-45

sports, 158-59

St. Louis, MO, vi

Stadem, Helge, 22

stalag, 95

Standard Beam Approach, 67

Station Hospital, 130

Stewart, Riley, 120

Stimson, Henry L., 49

Street, J.M., 33

Sub-Depot, 89

sugar, 169

Sunday dinners, 1, 13, 29-30, 193

**T**

taxi cabs, 139-40

Taylor, Olin (Jelly), 119-20

tear gas, 85

Techettes, 31, 153

Terrace Park pool, 106, 109, 113

thievery, 140

Thompson, Dr. Harry, vii

Thorstenson, Mark, 143

Thrond, Elizabeth, vii

tires, 137

Toledo, OH, vi

Town 'n Country Café, 35, 175

traffic fines, 137

transportation, 151-53

Travis, Brig. Gen. Robert F., 58, 189

Truman, Pres. Harry, 124, 185

Tuchman, Barbara, vi

**U**

U.S. Employment Service, 10, 91, 188

U. S. Public Health Service, 40

U.S. Treasury, 92

uniform of the day, 104-05

USO, 13-14, 31-34, 114, 190

Uthe, Douglas, vii

**V**

vagrancy, 139

vandalism, 139, 186

Vaughn, Bessie, 122

venereal disease, 37-41

Vermillion, SD, 26

Veterans Administration, 160

"Victory Gardens," 150, 173

"Victory Loans," 171

# W

Wall Lake, SD 35

War Department, 2, 4-7, 9, 15, 49, 89, 94, 178

*Ward-O-Scope*, 130

Warren, Louis, 64

"washbacks," 71

"washed out," 62

Washington High School, 188

Washington, D.C., 4, 183

Weaver, Maj. Gen. Walter, ix

weddings (local women), 36

Welk, Lawrence, 27, 176

West Point, 49

West, Lloyd F., 178

Western Union, 178

Whitfield, C. M., 6, 9, 11, 40, 137-38

Whitt, Mrs. John (Sylvia Ekeland), 125-26

Wiener, Morton, 67

Willy, Roy, 6

Wingler, Harold, 36, 108

women, 125-36

women (military), 132-36

Women's Army Corp (Women's Auxiliary Army Corps), 132, 134

Woods, Charlie, 114

Woods, M.T., 5-6

working in the cold, 102

Works Progress Administration (WPA), x, 17-18, 28

World War I, 86

# Y

YMCA, 13, 30, 33-34, 85

Young, Col. Sig R., 57

Yuma, AZ, 63